The Vision (

Dante Alighieri

(Translator: Henry Francis Cary)

Alpha Editions

This edition published in 2024

ISBN : 9789362990631

Design and Setting By
Alpha Editions
www.alphaedis.com
Email - info@alphaedis.com

As per information held with us this book is in Public Domain.
This book is a reproduction of an important historical work. Alpha Editions uses the best technology to reproduce historical work in the same manner it was first published to preserve its original nature. Any marks or number seen are left intentionally to preserve its true form.

Contents

CANTO I .... - 1 -
CANTO II .... - 8 -
CANTO III .... - 13 -
CANTO IV .... - 19 -
CANTO V .... - 25 -
CANTO VI .... - 34 -
CANTO VII .... - 39 -
CANTO VIII .... - 44 -
CANTO IX .... - 50 -
CANTO X .... - 56 -
CANTO XI .... - 61 -
CANTO XII .... - 65 -
CANTO XIII .... - 72 -
CANTO XIV .... - 78 -
CANTO XV .... - 83 -
CANTO XVI .... - 88 -
CANTO XVII .... - 92 -
CANTO XVIII .... - 97 -
CANTO XIX .... - 103 -
CANTO XX .... - 108 -
CANTO XXI .... - 112 -
CANTO XXII .... - 117 -
CANTO XXIII .... - 122 -
CANTO XXIV .... - 129 -
CANTO XXV .... - 134 -
CANTO XXVI .... - 139 -

CANTO XVII	- 144 -
CANTO XXVIII	- 148 -
CANTO XXIX	- 155 -
CANTO XXX	- 161 -
CANTO XXXI	- 167 -
CANTO XXXII	- 173 -
CANTO XXXIII	- 179 -
CANTO XXXIV	- 185 -

CANTO I

    In the midway of this our mortal life,
I found me in a gloomy wood, astray
Gone from the path direct: and e'en to tell
It were no easy task, how savage wild
That forest, how robust and rough its growth,
Which to remember only, my dismay
Renews, in bitterness not far from death.
Yet to discourse of what there good befell,
All else will I relate discover'd there.
How first I enter'd it I scarce can say,
Such sleepy dullness in that instant weigh'd
My senses down, when the true path I left,
But when a mountain's foot I reach'd, where clos'd

The valley, that had pierc'd my heart with dread,
I look'd aloft, and saw his shoulders broad
Already vested with that planet's beam,
Who leads all wanderers safe through every way.

Then was a little respite to the fear,
That in my heart's recesses deep had lain,
All of that night, so pitifully pass'd:
And as a man, with difficult short breath,
Forespent with toiling, 'scap'd from sea to shore,
Turns to the perilous wide waste, and stands
At gaze; e'en so my spirit, that yet fail'd
Struggling with terror, turn'd to view the straits,
That none hath pass'd and liv'd. My weary frame
After short pause recomforted, again
I journey'd on over that lonely steep,

> Scarce the ascent
> Began, when, lo! a panther, nimble, light,
> And cover'd with a speckled skin, appear'd;
> Nor, when it saw me, vanish'd.
> Canto I., lines 29—32.

    The hinder foot still firmer. Scarce the ascent
Began, when, lo! a panther, nimble, light,
And cover'd with a speckled skin, appear'd,
Nor, when it saw me, vanish'd, rather strove
To check my onward going; that ofttimes

With purpose to retrace my steps I turn'd.

The hour was morning's prime, and on his way
Aloft the sun ascended with those stars,
That with him rose, when Love divine first mov'd
Those its fair works: so that with joyous hope
All things conspir'd to fill me, the gay skin
Of that swift animal, the matin dawn
And the sweet season. Soon that joy was chas'd,
And by new dread succeeded, when in view
A lion came, 'gainst me, as it appear'd,

*A lion came, 'gainst me as it appear'd,
With his head held aloft, and hunger-mad.
Canto I., lines 43: 44*

With his head held aloft and hunger-mad,
That e'en the air was fear-struck. A she-wolf

Was at his heels, who in her leanness seem'd
Full of all wants, and many a land hath made
Disconsolate ere now. She with such fear
O'erwhelmed me, at the sight of her appall'd,
That of the height all hope I lost. As one,
Who with his gain elated, sees the time
When all unwares is gone, he inwardly
Mourns with heart-griping anguish; such was I,
Haunted by that fell beast, never at peace,
Who coming o'er against me, by degrees
Impell'd me where the sun in silence rests.

While to the lower space with backward step
I fell, my ken discern'd the form one of one,
Whose voice seem'd faint through long disuse of speech.
When him in that great desert I espied,
"Have mercy on me!" cried I out aloud,
"Spirit! or living man! what e'er thou be!"

He answer'd: "Now not man, man once I was,
And born of Lombard parents, Mantuana both
By country, when the power of Julius yet
Was scarcely firm. At Rome my life was past
Beneath the mild Augustus, in the time
Of fabled deities and false. A bard
Was I, and made Anchises' upright son
The subject of my song, who came from Troy,
When the flames prey'd on Ilium's haughty towers.
But thou, say wherefore to such perils past
Return'st thou? wherefore not this pleasant mount
Ascendest, cause and source of all delight?"
"And art thou then that Virgil, that well-spring,
From which such copious floods of eloquence
Have issued?" I with front abash'd replied.
"Glory and light of all the tuneful train!
May it avail me that I long with zeal
Have sought thy volume, and with love immense
Have conn'd it o'er. My master thou and guide!
Thou he from whom alone I have deriv'd
That style, which for its beauty into fame
Exalts me. See the beast, from whom I fled.
O save me from her, thou illustrious sage!

> He, soon as he saw
> That I was weeping, answer'd.
> Canto I., lines 87, 88.

"For every vein and pulse throughout my frame
She hath made tremble." He, soon as he saw
That I was weeping, answer'd, "Thou must needs
Another way pursue, if thou wouldst 'scape
From out that savage wilderness. This beast,
At whom thou criest, her way will suffer none
To pass, and no less hindrance makes than death:
So bad and so accursed in her kind,
That never sated is her ravenous will,
Still after food more craving than before.
To many an animal in wedlock vile

She fastens, and shall yet to many more,
Until that greyhound come, who shall destroy
Her with sharp pain. He will not life support
By earth nor its base metals, but by love,
Wisdom, and virtue, and his land shall be
The land 'twixt either Feltro. In his might
Shall safety to Italia's plains arise,
For whose fair realm, Camilla, virgin pure,
Nisus, Euryalus, and Turnus fell.
He with incessant chase through every town
Shall worry, until he to hell at length
Restore her, thence by envy first let loose.
I for thy profit pond'ring now devise,
That thou mayst follow me, and I thy guide
Will lead thee hence through an eternal space,
Where thou shalt hear despairing shrieks, and see
Spirits of old tormented, who invoke
A second death; and those next view, who dwell
Content in fire, for that they hope to come,
Whene'er the time may be, among the blest,
Into whose regions if thou then desire
T' ascend, a spirit worthier than I
Must lead thee, in whose charge, when I depart,
Thou shalt be left: for that Almighty King,
Who reigns above, a rebel to his law,
Adjudges me, and therefore hath decreed,
That to his city none through me should come.
He in all parts hath sway; there rules, there holds
His citadel and throne. O happy those,
Whom there he chooses!" I to him in few:
"Bard! by that God, whom thou didst not adore,
I do beseech thee (that this ill and worse
I may escape) to lead me, where thou saidst,
That I Saint Peter's gate may view, and those
Who as thou tell'st, are in such dismal plight."

Onward he mov'd, I close his steps pursu'd.

Onward he moved, I close his steps pursued.
Canto I., line 132.

CANTO II

Now was the day departing, and the air,
Imbrown'd with shadows, from their toils releas'd
All animals on earth; and I alone
Prepar'd myself the conflict to sustain,
Both of sad pity, and that perilous road,
Which my unerring memory shall retrace.

O Muses! O high genius! now vouchsafe
Your aid! O mind! that all I saw hast kept
Safe in a written record, here thy worth
And eminent endowments come to proof.

I thus began: "Bard! thou who art my guide,
Consider well, if virtue be in me

Sufficient, ere to this high enterprise
Thou trust me. Thou hast told that Silvius' sire,
Yet cloth'd in corruptible flesh, among
Th' immortal tribes had entrance, and was there
Sensible present. Yet if heaven's great Lord,
Almighty foe to ill, such favour shew'd,
In contemplation of the high effect,
Both what and who from him should issue forth,
It seems in reason's judgment well deserv'd:
Sith he of Rome, and of Rome's empire wide,
In heaven's empyreal height was chosen sire:
Both which, if truth be spoken, were ordain'd
And 'stablish'd for the holy place, where sits
Who to great Peter's sacred chair succeeds.
He from this journey, in thy song renown'd,
Learn'd things, that to his victory gave rise
And to the papal robe. In after-times
The chosen vessel also travel'd there,
To bring us back assurance in that faith,
Which is the entrance to salvation's way.
But I, why should I there presume? or who
Permits it? not Aeneas I nor Paul.
Myself I deem not worthy, and none else
Will deem me. I, if on this voyage then
I venture, fear it will in folly end.
Thou, who art wise, better my meaning know'st,
Than I can speak." As one, who unresolves
What he hath late resolv'd, and with new thoughts
Changes his purpose, from his first intent
Remov'd; e'en such was I on that dun coast,
Wasting in thought my enterprise, at first
So eagerly embrac'd. "If right thy words
I scan," replied that shade magnanimous,
"Thy soul is by vile fear assail'd, which oft
So overcasts a man, that he recoils
From noblest resolution, like a beast
At some false semblance in the twilight gloom.
That from this terror thou mayst free thyself,
I will instruct thee why I came, and what
I heard in that same instant, when for thee
Grief touch'd me first. I was among the tribe,
Who rest suspended, when a dame, so blest
And lovely, I besought her to command,

Call'd me; her eyes were brighter than the star
Of day; and she with gentle voice and soft
Angelically tun'd her speech address'd:
"O courteous shade of Mantua! thou whose fame
Yet lives, and shall live long as nature lasts!
A friend, not of my fortune but myself,
On the wide desert in his road has met
Hindrance so great, that he through fear has turn'd.
Now much I dread lest he past help have stray'd,
And I be ris'n too late for his relief,
From what in heaven of him I heard. Speed now,
And by thy eloquent persuasive tongue,
And by all means for his deliverance meet,
Assist him. So to me will comfort spring.
I who now bid thee on this errand forth
Am Beatrice; from a place I come.

(Note: Beatrice. I use this word, as it is
pronounced in the Italian, as consisting of four
syllables, of which the third is a long one.) Revisited with joy. Love brought me thence,
Who prompts my speech. When in my Master's sight
I stand, thy praise to him I oft will tell."

She then was silent, and I thus began:
"O Lady! by whose influence alone,
Mankind excels whatever is contain'd
Within that heaven which hath the smallest orb,
So thy command delights me, that to obey,
If it were done already, would seem late.
No need hast thou farther to speak thy will;
Yet tell the reason, why thou art not loth
To leave that ample space, where to return
Thou burnest, for this centre here beneath."

She then: "Since thou so deeply wouldst inquire,
I will instruct thee briefly, why no dread
Hinders my entrance here. Those things alone
Are to be fear'd, whence evil may proceed,
None else, for none are terrible beside.
I am so fram'd by God, thanks to his grace!
That any suff'rance of your misery
Touches me not, nor flame of that fierce fire
Assails me. In high heaven a blessed dame
Besides, who mourns with such effectual grief
That hindrance, which I send thee to remove,
That God's stern judgment to her will inclines."
To Lucia calling, her she thus bespake:
"Now doth thy faithful servant need thy aid
And I commend him to thee." At her word
Sped Lucia, of all cruelty the foe,
And coming to the place, where I abode
Seated with Rachel, her of ancient days,
She thus address'd me: "Thou true praise of God!
Beatrice! why is not thy succour lent
To him, who so much lov'd thee, as to leave
For thy sake all the multitude admires?
Dost thou not hear how pitiful his wail,
Nor mark the death, which in the torrent flood,
Swoln mightier than a sea, him struggling holds?"

Ne'er among men did any with such speed
Haste to their profit, flee from their annoy,
As when these words were spoken, I came here,
Down from my blessed seat, trusting the force
Of thy pure eloquence, which thee, and all
Who well have mark'd it, into honour brings."

"When she had ended, her bright beaming eyes
Tearful she turn'd aside; whereat I felt
Redoubled zeal to serve thee. As she will'd,
Thus am I come: I sav'd thee from the beast,
Who thy near way across the goodly mount
Prevented. What is this comes o'er thee then?
Why, why dost thou hang back? why in thy breast
Harbour vile fear? why hast not courage there
And noble daring? Since three maids so blest
Thy safety plan, e'en in the court of heaven;
And so much certain good my words forebode."

As florets, by the frosty air of night
Bent down and clos'd, when day has blanch'd their leaves,
Rise all unfolded on their spiry stems;
So was my fainting vigour new restor'd,
And to my heart such kindly courage ran,
That I as one undaunted soon replied:
"O full of pity she, who undertook
My succour! and thou kind who didst perform
So soon her true behest! With such desire
Thou hast dispos'd me to renew my voyage,
That my first purpose fully is resum'd.
Lead on: one only will is in us both.
Thou art my guide, my master thou, and lord."

So spake I; and when he had onward mov'd,
I enter'd on the deep and woody way.

CANTO III

"Through me you pass into the city of woe:
Through me you pass into eternal pain:
Through me among the people lost for aye.
Justice the founder of my fabric mov'd:
To rear me was the task of power divine,
Supremest wisdom, and primeval love.
Before me things create were none, save things
Eternal, and eternal I endure.

"All hope abandon ye who enter here."

Such characters in colour dim I mark'd
Over a portal's lofty arch inscrib'd:
Whereat I thus: "Master, these words import
Hard meaning." He as one prepar'd replied:
"Here thou must all distrust behind thee leave;
Here be vile fear extinguish'd. We are come
Where I have told thee we shall see the souls
To misery doom'd, who intellectual good
Have lost." And when his hand he had stretch'd forth
To mine, with pleasant looks, whence I was cheer'd,

Into that secret place he led me on.

Here sighs with lamentations and loud moans
Resounded through the air pierc'd by no star,
That e'en I wept at entering. Various tongues,
Horrible languages, outcries of woe,
Accents of anger, voices deep and hoarse,
With hands together smote that swell'd the sounds,
Made up a tumult, that for ever whirls
Round through that air with solid darkness stain'd,
Like to the sand that in the whirlwind flies.

I then, with error yet encompass'd, cried:
"O master! What is this I hear? What race
Are these, who seem so overcome with woe?"

He thus to me: "This miserable fate
Suffer the wretched souls of those, who liv'd
Without or praise or blame, with that ill band
Of angels mix'd, who nor rebellious prov'd
Nor yet were true to God, but for themselves
Were only. From his bounds Heaven drove them forth,
Not to impair his lustre, nor the depth
Of Hell receives them, lest th' accursed tribe
Should glory thence with exultation vain."

I then: "Master! what doth aggrieve them thus,
That they lament so loud?" He straight replied:
"That will I tell thee briefly. These of death
No hope may entertain: and their blind life
So meanly passes, that all other lots
They envy. Fame of them the world hath none,
Nor suffers; mercy and justice scorn them both.
Speak not of them, but look, and pass them by."

And I, who straightway look'd, beheld a flag,
Which whirling ran around so rapidly,
That it no pause obtain'd: and following came
Such a long train of spirits, I should ne'er
Have thought, that death so many had despoil'd.

When some of these I recogniz'd, I saw
And knew the shade of him, who to base fear

Yielding, abjur'd his high estate. Forthwith
I understood for certain this the tribe
Of those ill spirits both to God displeasing
And to his foes. These wretches, who ne'er lived,
Went on in nakedness, and sorely stung
By wasps and hornets, which bedew'd their cheeks
With blood, that mix'd with tears dropp'd to their feet,
And by disgustful worms was gather'd there.

Then looking farther onwards I beheld
A throng upon the shore of a great stream:
Whereat I thus: "Sir! grant me now to know
Whom here we view, and whence impell'd they seem
So eager to pass o'er, as I discern
Through the blear light?" He thus to me in few:
"This shalt thou know, soon as our steps arrive
Beside the woeful tide of Acheron."

Then with eyes downward cast and fill'd with shame,
Fearing my words offensive to his ear,
Till we had reach'd the river, I from speech
Abstain'd. And lo! toward us in a bark
Comes on an old man hoary white with eld,

> And, lo! toward us in a bark
> Comes on an old man, hoary white with eld,
> Crying, "Woe to you, wicked spirits!"
> *Canto III, lines 76—78*

    Crying, "Woe to you wicked spirits! hope not
Ever to see the sky again. I come
To take you to the other shore across,
Into eternal darkness, there to dwell
In fierce heat and in ice. And thou, who there
Standest, live spirit! get thee hence, and leave
These who are dead." But soon as he beheld
I left them not, "By other way," said he,
"By other haven shalt thou come to shore,
Not by this passage; thee a nimbler boat
Must carry." Then to him thus spake my guide:
"Charon! thyself torment not: so 't is will'd,
Where will and power are one: ask thou no more."

Straightway in silence fell the shaggy cheeks

Of him the boatman o'er the livid lake,
Around whose eyes glar'd wheeling flames. Meanwhile
Those spirits, faint and naked, color chang'd,
And gnash'd their teeth, soon as the cruel words
They heard. God and their parents they blasphem'd,
The human kind, the place, the time, and seed
That did engender them and give them birth.

Then all together sorely wailing drew
To the curs'd strand, that every man must pass
Who fears not God. Charon, demoniac form,
With eyes of burning coal, collects them all,
Beck'ning, and each, that lingers, with his oar
Strikes. As fall off the light autumnal leaves,
One still another following, till the bough
Strews all its honours on the earth beneath;

E'en in like manner Adam's evil brood
Cast themselves, one by one, down from the shore.
Canto III., lines 107, 108.

    E'en in like manner Adam's evil brood
Cast themselves one by one down from the shore,
Each at a beck, as falcon at his call.

Thus go they over through the umber'd wave,

And ever they on the opposing bank
Be landed, on this side another throng
Still gathers. "Son," thus spake the courteous guide,
"Those, who die subject to the wrath of God,
All here together come from every clime,
And to o'erpass the river are not loth:
For so heaven's justice goads them on, that fear
Is turn'd into desire. Hence ne'er hath past
Good spirit. If of thee Charon complain,
Now mayst thou know the import of his words."

This said, the gloomy region trembling shook
So terribly, that yet with clammy dews
Fear chills my brow. The sad earth gave a blast,
That, lightening, shot forth a vermilion flame,
Which all my senses conquer'd quite, and I
Down dropp'd, as one with sudden slumber seiz'd.

CANTO IV

    Broke the deep slumber in my brain a crash
Of heavy thunder, that I shook myself,
As one by main force rous'd. Risen upright,
My rested eyes I mov'd around, and search'd
With fixed ken to know what place it was,
Wherein I stood. For certain on the brink
I found me of the lamentable vale,
The dread abyss, that joins a thund'rous sound
Of plaints innumerable. Dark and deep,
And thick with clouds o'erspread, mine eye in vain
Explor'd its bottom, nor could aught discern.

"Now let us to the blind world there beneath
Descend;" the bard began all pale of look:
"I go the first, and thou shalt follow next."

Then I his alter'd hue perceiving, thus:
"How may I speed, if thou yieldest to dread,
Who still art wont to comfort me in doubt?"

He then: "The anguish of that race below
With pity stains my cheek, which thou for fear
Mistakest. Let us on. Our length of way
Urges to haste." Onward, this said, he mov'd;
And ent'ring led me with him on the bounds
Of the first circle, that surrounds th' abyss.
Here, as mine ear could note, no plaint was heard
Except of sighs, that made th' eternal air
Tremble, not caus'd by tortures, but from grief
Felt by those multitudes, many and vast,
Of men, women, and infants. Then to me
The gentle guide: "Inquir'st thou not what spirits
Are these, which thou beholdest? Ere thou pass
Farther, I would thou know, that these of sin
Were blameless; and if aught they merited,
It profits not, since baptism was not theirs,
The portal to thy faith. If they before
The Gospel liv'd, they serv'd not God aright;
And among such am I. For these defects,
And for no other evil, we are lost;

"Only so far afflicted, that we live
Desiring without hope." So grief assail'd
My heart at hearing this, for well I knew
Suspended in that Limbo many a soul
Of mighty worth. "O tell me, sire rever'd!
Tell me, my master!" I began through wish
Of full assurance in that holy faith,
Which vanquishes all error; "say, did e'er
Any, or through his own or other's merit,
Come forth from thence, whom afterward was blest?"

Piercing the secret purport of my speech,
He answer'd: "I was new to that estate,
When I beheld a puissant one arrive
Amongst us, with victorious trophy crown'd.
He forth the shade of our first parent drew,
Abel his child, and Noah righteous man,
Of Moses lawgiver for faith approv'd,
Of patriarch Abraham, and David king,
Israel with his sire and with his sons,
Nor without Rachel whom so hard he won,
And others many more, whom he to bliss

Exalted. Before these, be thou assur'd,
No spirit of human kind was ever sav'd."

We, while he spake, ceas'd not our onward road,
Still passing through the wood; for so I name
Those spirits thick beset. We were not far
On this side from the summit, when I kenn'd
A flame, that o'er the darken'd hemisphere
Prevailing shin'd. Yet we a little space
Were distant, not so far but I in part
Discover'd, that a tribe in honour high
That place possess'd. "O thou, who every art
And science valu'st! who are these, that boast
Such honour, separate from all the rest?"

He answer'd: "The renown of their great names
That echoes through your world above, acquires
Favour in heaven, which holds them thus advanc'd."
Meantime a voice I heard: "Honour the bard
Sublime! his shade returns that left us late!"
No sooner ceas'd the sound, than I beheld
Four mighty spirits toward us bend their steps,
Of semblance neither sorrowful nor glad.

When thus my master kind began: "Mark him,
Who in his right hand bears that falchion keen,
The other three preceding, as their lord.
This is that Homer, of all bards supreme:
Flaccus the next in satire's vein excelling;
The third is Naso; Lucan is the last.
Because they all that appellation own,
With which the voice singly accosted me,
Honouring they greet me thus, and well they judge."

So I beheld united the bright school
Of him the monarch of sublimest song,
That o'er the others like an eagle soars.
When they together short discourse had held,
They turn'd to me, with salutation kind
Beck'ning me; at the which my master smil'd:
Nor was this all; but greater honour still
They gave me, for they made me of their tribe;
And I was sixth amid so learn'd a band.

Far as the luminous beacon on we pass'd
Speaking of matters, then befitting well
To speak, now fitter left untold. At foot
Of a magnificent castle we arriv'd,
Seven times with lofty walls begirt, and round
Defended by a pleasant stream. O'er this

As o'er dry land we pass'd. Next through seven gates
I with those sages enter'd, and we came
Into a mead with lively verdure fresh.

There dwelt a race, who slow their eyes around
Majestically mov'd, and in their port
Bore eminent authority; they spake
Seldom, but all their words were tuneful sweet.

We to one side retir'd, into a place
Open and bright and lofty, whence each one
Stood manifest to view. Incontinent
There on the green enamel of the plain
Were shown me the great spirits, by whose sight
I am exalted in my own esteem.

Electra there I saw accompanied
By many, among whom Hector I knew,
Anchises' pious son, and with hawk's eye
Caesar all arm'd, and by Camilla there
Penthesilea. On the other side
Old King Latinus, seated by his child
Lavinia, and that Brutus I beheld,
Who Tarquin chas'd, Lucretia, Cato's wife
Marcia, with Julia and Cornelia there;
And sole apart retir'd, the Soldan fierce.

Then when a little more I rais'd my brow,
I spied the master of the sapient throng,
Seated amid the philosophic train.
Him all admire, all pay him rev'rence due.
There Socrates and Plato both I mark'd,
Nearest to him in rank; Democritus,
Who sets the world at chance, Diogenes,
With Heraclitus, and Empedocles,
And Anaxagoras, and Thales sage,
Zeno, and Dioscorides well read
In nature's secret lore. Orpheus I mark'd
And Linus, Tully and moral Seneca,
Euclid and Ptolemy, Hippocrates,
Galenus, Avicen, and him who made
That commentary vast, Averroes.

Of all to speak at full were vain attempt;
For my wide theme so urges, that ofttimes
My words fall short of what bechanc'd. In two
The six associates part. Another way
My sage guide leads me, from that air serene,
Into a climate ever vex'd with storms:
And to a part I come where no light shines.

CANTO V

From the first circle I descended thus
Down to the second, which, a lesser space
Embracing, so much more of grief contains
Provoking bitter moans. There, Minos stands
Grinning with ghastly feature: he, of all
Who enter, strict examining the crimes,

There Minos stands. Canto V, line 4.

Gives sentence, and dismisses them beneath,
According as he foldeth him around:
For when before him comes th' ill fated soul,
It all confesses; and that judge severe
Of sins, considering what place in hell
Suits the transgression, with his tail so oft
Himself encircles, as degrees beneath
He dooms it to descend. Before him stand
Always a num'rous throng; and in his turn
Each one to judgment passing, speaks, and hears
His fate, thence downward to his dwelling hurl'd.

"O thou! who to this residence of woe
Approachest?" when he saw me coming, cried

Minos, relinquishing his dread employ,
"Look how thou enter here; beware in whom
Thou place thy trust; let not the entrance broad
Deceive thee to thy harm." To him my guide:
"Wherefore exclaimest? Hinder not his way
By destiny appointed; so 'tis will'd
Where will and power are one. Ask thou no more."

Now 'gin the rueful wailings to be heard.
Now am I come where many a plaining voice
Smites on mine ear. Into a place I came
Where light was silent all. Bellowing there groan'd
A noise as of a sea in tempest torn
By warring winds. The stormy blast of hell
With restless fury drives the spirits on
Whirl'd round and dash'd amain with sore annoy.

*The stormy blast of hell
With restless fury drives the spirits on.
Canto V., lines 32, 33.*

    When they arrive before the ruinous sweep,
There shrieks are heard, there lamentations, moans,
And blasphemies 'gainst the good Power in heaven.

I understood that to this torment sad
The carnal sinners are condemn'd, in whom
Reason by lust is sway'd. As in large troops
And multitudinous, when winter reigns,
The starlings on their wings are borne abroad;
So bears the tyrannous gust those evil souls.
On this side and on that, above, below,
It drives them: hope of rest to solace them
Is none, nor e'en of milder pang. As cranes,
Chanting their dol'rous notes, traverse the sky,

Stretch'd out in long array: so I beheld
Spirits, who came loud wailing, hurried on
By their dire doom. Then I: "Instructor! who
Are these, by the black air so scourg'd?"—"The first
'Mong those, of whom thou question'st," he replied,
"O'er many tongues was empress. She in vice
Of luxury was so shameless, that she made
Liking be lawful by promulg'd decree,
To clear the blame she had herself incurr'd.
This is Semiramis, of whom 'tis writ,
That she succeeded Ninus her espous'd;
And held the land, which now the Soldan rules.
The next in amorous fury slew herself,
And to Sicheus' ashes broke her faith:
Then follows Cleopatra, lustful queen."

There mark'd I Helen, for whose sake so long
The time was fraught with evil; there the great
Achilles, who with love fought to the end.
Paris I saw, and Tristan; and beside
A thousand more he show'd me, and by name
Pointed them out, whom love bereav'd of life.

When I had heard my sage instructor name
Those dames and knights of antique days, o'erpower'd
By pity, well-nigh in amaze my mind
Was lost; and I began: "Bard! willingly
I would address those two together coming,
Which seem so light before the wind." He thus:
"Note thou, when nearer they to us approach.

*Hard! willingly
I would address those two together coming,
Which seem so light before the wind.*
Canto V., lines 72—74.

"Then by that love which carries them along,
Entreat; and they will come." Soon as the wind
Sway'd them toward us, I thus fram'd my speech:
"O wearied spirits! come, and hold discourse
With us, if by none else restrain'd." As doves
By fond desire invited, on wide wings
And firm, to their sweet nest returning home,
Cleave the air, wafted by their will along;
Thus issu'd from that troop, where Dido ranks,
They through the ill air speeding; with such force
My cry prevail'd by strong affection urg'd.

"O gracious creature and benign! who go'st

Visiting, through this element obscure,
Us, who the world with bloody stain imbru'd;
If for a friend the King of all we own'd,
Our pray'r to him should for thy peace arise,
Since thou hast pity on our evil plight.
Of whatsoe'er to hear or to discourse
It pleases thee, that will we hear, of that
Freely with thee discourse, while e'er the wind,
As now, is mute. The land, that gave me birth,
Is situate on the coast, where Po descends
To rest in ocean with his sequent streams.

"Love, that in gentle heart is quickly learnt,
Entangled him by that fair form, from me
Ta'en in such cruel sort, as grieves me still:
Love, that denial takes from none belov'd,
Caught me with pleasing him so passing well,
That, as thou see'st, he yet deserts me not.

Love brought us to one death: Caina waits
The soul who spilt our life.
Canto V., lines 105, 106.

"Love brought us to one death: Caina waits
The soul, who spilt our life." Such were their words;
At hearing which downward I bent my looks,

And held them there so long, that the bard cried:
"What art thou pond'ring?" I in answer thus:
"Alas! by what sweet thoughts, what fond desire
Must they at length to that ill pass have reach'd!"

Then turning, I to them my speech address'd.
And thus began: "Francesca! your sad fate
Even to tears my grief and pity moves.
But tell me; in the time of your sweet sighs,
By what, and how love granted, that ye knew
Your yet uncertain wishes?" She replied:
"No greater grief than to remember days
Of joy, when mis'ry is at hand! That kens
Thy learn'd instructor. Yet so eagerly
If thou art bent to know the primal root,
From whence our love gat being, I will do,
As one, who weeps and tells his tale. One day
For our delight we read of Lancelot,
How him love thrall'd. Alone we were, and no
Suspicion near us. Ofttimes by that reading
Our eyes were drawn together, and the hue
Fled from our alter'd cheek. But at one point
Alone we fell. When of that smile we read,
The wished smile, rapturously kiss'd
By one so deep in love, then he, who ne'er
From me shall separate, at once my lips
All trembling kiss'd. The book and writer both
Were love's purveyors. In its leaves that day
We read no more." While thus one spirit spake,
The other wail'd so sorely, that heartstruck
I through compassion fainting, seem'd not far
From death, and like a corpse fell to the ground.

In its leaves that day
We read no more.
Canto V., lines 134, 135.

I, through compassion fainting, seem'd not far
From death, and like a corse fell to the ground.
Canto V., lines 137, 138.

CANTO VI

    My sense reviving, that erewhile had droop'd
With pity for the kindred shades, whence grief
O'ercame me wholly, straight around I see
New torments, new tormented souls, which way
Soe'er I move, or turn, or bend my sight.
In the third circle I arrive, of show'rs
Ceaseless, accursed, heavy, and cold, unchang'd
For ever, both in kind and in degree.
Large hail, discolour'd water, sleety flaw
Through the dun midnight air stream'd down amain:
Stank all the land whereon that tempest fell.

Cerberus, cruel monster, fierce and strange,
Through his wide threefold throat barks as a dog
Over the multitude immers'd beneath.
His eyes glare crimson, black his unctuous beard,
His belly large, and claw'd the hands, with which
He tears the spirits, flays them, and their limbs
Piecemeal disparts. Howling there spread, as curs,
Under the rainy deluge, with one side
The other screening, oft they roll them round,
A wretched, godless crew. When that great worm
Descried us, savage Cerberus, he op'd
His jaws, and the fangs show'd us; not a limb
Of him but trembled. Then my guide, his palms
Expanding on the ground, thence filled with earth
Rais'd them, and cast it in his ravenous maw.

E'en as a dog, that yelling bays for food
His keeper, when the morsel comes, lets fall
His fury, bent alone with eager haste
To swallow it; so dropp'd the loathsome cheeks
Of demon Cerberus, who thund'ring stuns
The spirits, that they for deafness wish in vain.

We, o'er the shades thrown prostrate by the brunt
Of the heavy tempest passing, set our feet
Upon their emptiness, that substance seem'd.

They all along the earth extended lay
Save one, that sudden rais'd himself to sit,
Soon as that way he saw us pass. "O thou!"
He cried, "who through the infernal shades art led,
Own, if again thou know'st me. Thou wast fram'd
Or ere my frame was broken." I replied:
"The anguish thou endur'st perchance so takes
Thy form from my remembrance, that it seems
As if I saw thee never. But inform
Me who thou art, that in a place so sad
Art set, and in such torment, that although

Other be greater, more disgustful none
Can be imagin'd." He in answer thus:

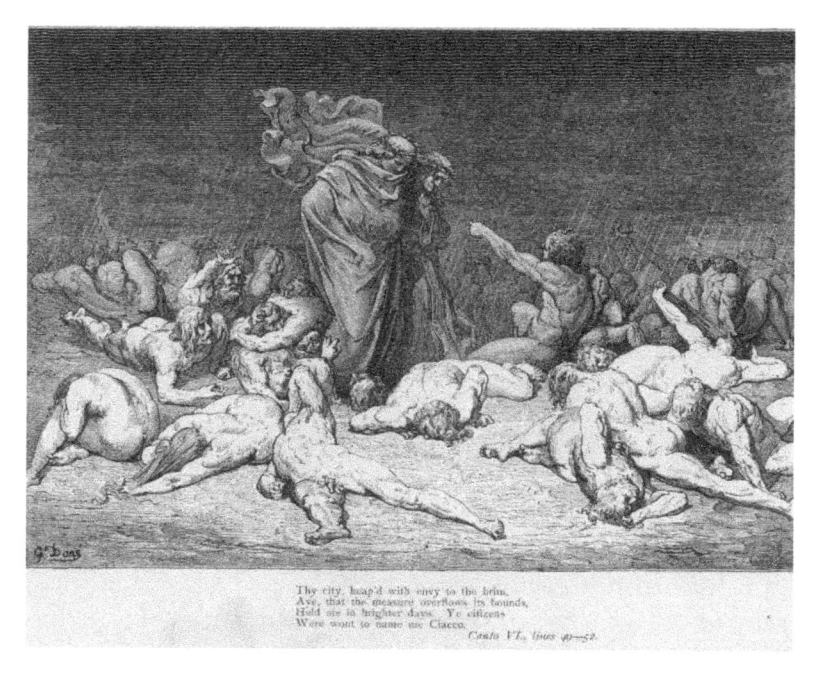

"Thy city heap'd with envy to the brim,
Ay that the measure overflows its bounds,
Held me in brighter days. Ye citizens
Were wont to name me Ciacco. For the sin
Of glutt'ny, damned vice, beneath this rain,
E'en as thou see'st, I with fatigue am worn;
Nor I sole spirit in this woe: all these
Have by like crime incurr'd like punishment."

No more he said, and I my speech resum'd:
"Ciacco! thy dire affliction grieves me much,
Even to tears. But tell me, if thou know'st,
What shall at length befall the citizens
Of the divided city; whether any just one
Inhabit there: and tell me of the cause,
Whence jarring discord hath assail'd it thus?"

He then: "After long striving they will come
To blood; and the wild party from the woods
Will chase the other with much injury forth.

Then it behoves, that this must fall, within
Three solar circles; and the other rise
By borrow'd force of one, who under shore
Now rests. It shall a long space hold aloof
Its forehead, keeping under heavy weight
The other oppress'd, indignant at the load,
And grieving sore. The just are two in number,
But they neglected. Av'rice, envy, pride,
Three fatal sparks, have set the hearts of all
On fire." Here ceas'd the lamentable sound;
And I continu'd thus: "Still would I learn
More from thee, farther parley still entreat.
Of Farinata and Tegghiaio say,
They who so well deserv'd, of Giacopo,
Arrigo, Mosca, and the rest, who bent
Their minds on working good. Oh! tell me where
They bide, and to their knowledge let me come.
For I am press'd with keen desire to hear,
If heaven's sweet cup or poisonous drug of hell
Be to their lip assign'd." He answer'd straight:
"These are yet blacker spirits. Various crimes
Have sunk them deeper in the dark abyss.
If thou so far descendest, thou mayst see them.
But to the pleasant world when thou return'st,
Of me make mention, I entreat thee, there.
No more I tell thee, answer thee no more."

This said, his fixed eyes he turn'd askance,
A little ey'd me, then bent down his head,
And 'midst his blind companions with it fell.

When thus my guide: "No more his bed he leaves,
Ere the last angel-trumpet blow. The Power
Adverse to these shall then in glory come,
Each one forthwith to his sad tomb repair,
Resume his fleshly vesture and his form,
And hear the eternal doom re-echoing rend
The vault." So pass'd we through that mixture foul
Of spirits and rain, with tardy steps; meanwhile
Touching, though slightly, on the life to come.
For thus I question'd: "Shall these tortures, Sir!
When the great sentence passes, be increas'd,
Or mitigated, or as now severe?"

He then: "Consult thy knowledge; that decides
That as each thing to more perfection grows,
It feels more sensibly both good and pain.
Though ne'er to true perfection may arrive
This race accurs'd, yet nearer then than now
They shall approach it." Compassing that path
Circuitous we journeyed, and discourse
Much more than I relate between us pass'd:
Till at the point, where the steps led below,
Arriv'd, there Plutus, the great foe, we found.

CANTO VII

"Ah me! O Satan! Satan!" loud exclaim'd
Plutus, in accent hoarse of wild alarm:
And the kind sage, whom no event surpris'd,
To comfort me thus spake: "Let not thy fear
Harm thee, for power in him, be sure, is none
To hinder down this rock thy safe descent."
Then to that sworn lip turning, "Peace!" he cried,

Curs'd wolf! thy fury inward on thyself
Prey; and consume thee!
Canto VII, lines 8, 9

"Curs'd wolf! thy fury inward on thyself
Prey, and consume thee! Through the dark profound
Not without cause he passes. So 't is will'd
On high, there where the great Archangel pour'd
Heav'n's vengeance on the first adulterer proud."

As sails full spread and bellying with the wind
Drop suddenly collaps'd, if the mast split;
So to the ground down dropp'd the cruel fiend.

Thus we, descending to the fourth steep ledge,
Gain'd on the dismal shore, that all the woe
Hems in of all the universe. Ah me!
Almighty Justice! in what store thou heap'st

New pains, new troubles, as I here beheld!
Wherefore doth fault of ours bring us to this?

E'en as a billow, on Charybdis rising,
Against encounter'd billow dashing breaks;
Such is the dance this wretched race must lead,
Whom more than elsewhere numerous here I found,
From one side and the other, with loud voice,
Both roll'd on weights by main forge of their breasts,
Then smote together, and each one forthwith
Roll'd them back voluble, turning again,
Exclaiming these, "Why holdest thou so fast?"
Those answering, "And why castest thou away?"
So still repeating their despiteful song,
They to the opposite point on either hand
Travers'd the horrid circle: then arriv'd,
Both turn'd them round, and through the middle space
Conflicting met again. At sight whereof
I, stung with grief, thus spake: "O say, my guide!
What race is this? Were these, whose heads are shorn,
On our left hand, all sep'rate to the church?"

He straight replied: "In their first life these all
In mind were so distorted, that they made,
According to due measure, of their wealth,
No use. This clearly from their words collect,
Which they howl forth, at each extremity
Arriving of the circle, where their crime
Contrary in kind disparts them. To the church
Were separate those, that with no hairy cowls
Are crown'd, both Popes and Cardinals, o'er whom
Av'rice dominion absolute maintains."

I then: "Mid such as these some needs must be,
Whom I shall recognize, that with the blot
Of these foul sins were stain'd." He answering thus:
"Vain thought conceiv'st thou. That ignoble life,
Which made them vile before, now makes them dark,
And to all knowledge indiscernible.
Forever they shall meet in this rude shock:
These from the tomb with clenched grasp shall rise,
Those with close-shaven locks. That ill they gave,
And ill they kept, hath of the beauteous world

Depriv'd, and set them at this strife, which needs
No labour'd phrase of mine to set it off.
Now may'st thou see, my son! how brief, how vain,
The goods committed into fortune's hands,
For which the human race keep such a coil!
Not all the gold, that is beneath the moon,
Or ever hath been, of these toil-worn souls
Might purchase rest for one." I thus rejoin'd:

"My guide! of thee this also would I learn;
This fortune, that thou speak'st of, what it is,
Whose talons grasp the blessings of the world?"

He thus: "O beings blind! what ignorance
Besets you? Now my judgment hear and mark.
He, whose transcendent wisdom passes all,
The heavens creating, gave them ruling powers
To guide them, so that each part shines to each,
Their light in equal distribution pour'd.
By similar appointment he ordain'd
Over the world's bright images to rule
Superintendence of a guiding hand
And general minister, which at due time

May change the empty vantages of life
From race to race, from one to other's blood,
Beyond prevention of man's wisest care:
Wherefore one nation rises into sway,
Another languishes, e'en as her will
Decrees, from us conceal'd, as in the grass
The serpent train. Against her nought avails
Your utmost wisdom. She with foresight plans,
Judges, and carries on her reign, as theirs
The other powers divine. Her changes know
None intermission: by necessity
She is made swift, so frequent come who claim
Succession in her favours. This is she,
So execrated e'en by those, whose debt
To her is rather praise; they wrongfully
With blame requite her, and with evil word;
But she is blessed, and for that recks not:
Amidst the other primal beings glad
Rolls on her sphere, and in her bliss exults.
Now on our way pass we, to heavier woe
Descending: for each star is falling now,
That mounted at our entrance, and forbids
Too long our tarrying." We the circle cross'd
To the next steep, arriving at a well,
That boiling pours itself down to a foss
Sluic'd from its source. Far murkier was the wave
Than sablest grain: and we in company
Of the inky waters, journeying by their side,
Enter'd, though by a different track, beneath.
Into a lake, the Stygian nam'd, expands
The dismal stream, when it hath reach'd the foot
Of the grey wither'd cliffs. Intent I stood
To gaze, and in the marish sunk descried
A miry tribe, all naked, and with looks
Betok'ning rage. They with their hands alone
Struck not, but with the head, the breast, the feet,
Cutting each other piecemeal with their fangs.

Now seest thou, son!
The souls of those, whom anger overcame.
Canto VII., lines 118, 119.

    The good instructor spake; "Now seest thou, son!
The souls of those, whom anger overcame.
This too for certain know, that underneath
The water dwells a multitude, whose sighs
Into these bubbles make the surface heave,
As thine eye tells thee wheresoe'er it turn.
Fix'd in the slime they say: 'Sad once were we
In the sweet air made gladsome by the sun,
Carrying a foul and lazy mist within:
Now in these murky settlings are we sad.'
Such dolorous strain they gurgle in their throats.
But word distinct can utter none." Our route
Thus compass'd we, a segment widely stretch'd
Between the dry embankment, and the core
Of the loath'd pool, turning meanwhile our eyes
Downward on those who gulp'd its muddy lees;
Nor stopp'd, till to a tower's low base we came.

CANTO VIII

    My theme pursuing, I relate that ere
We reach'd the lofty turret's base, our eyes
Its height ascended, where two cressets hung
We mark'd, and from afar another light
Return the signal, so remote, that scarce
The eye could catch its beam. I turning round
To the deep source of knowledge, thus inquir'd:
"Say what this means? and what that other light
In answer set? what agency doth this?"

"There on the filthy waters," he replied,
"E'en now what next awaits us mayst thou see,
If the marsh-gender'd fog conceal it not."

Never was arrow from the cord dismiss'd,
That ran its way so nimbly through the air,
As a small bark, that through the waves I spied
Toward us coming, under the sole sway
Of one that ferried it, who cried aloud:
"Art thou arriv'd, fell spirit?"—"Phlegyas, Phlegyas,
This time thou criest in vain," my lord replied;
"No longer shalt thou have us, but while o'er
The slimy pool we pass." As one who hears
Of some great wrong he hath sustain'd, whereat
Inly he pines; so Phlegyas inly pin'd
In his fierce ire. My guide descending stepp'd
Into the skiff, and bade me enter next
Close at his side; nor till my entrance seem'd
The vessel freighted. Soon as both embark'd,
Cutting the waves, goes on the ancient prow,
More deeply than with others it is wont.

> Soon as both embark'd,
> Cutting the waves, goes on the ancient prow,
> More deeply than with others it is wont.
> *Canto VIII., lines 27—29.*

While we our course o'er the dead channel held.
One drench'd in mire before me came, and said;
"Who art thou, that thou comest ere thine hour?"

I answer'd: "Though I come, I tarry not;
But who art thou, that art become so foul?"

"One, as thou seest, who mourn:" he straight replied.

To which I thus: "In mourning and in woe,
Curs'd spirit! tarry thou. I know thee well,
E'en thus in filth disguis'd." Then stretch'd he forth
Hands to the bark; whereof my teacher sage
Aware, thrusting him back: "Away! down there,

*My teacher sage
Aware, thrusting him back: "Away! down there
To the other dogs!"*

Canto VIII, lines 39—41.

"To the other dogs!" then, with his arms my neck
Encircling, kiss'd my cheek, and spake: "O soul
Justly disdainful! blest was she in whom
Thou was conceiv'd! He in the world was one
For arrogance noted; to his memory
No virtue lends its lustre; even so
Here is his shadow furious. There above
How many now hold themselves mighty kings
Who here like swine shall wallow in the mire,
Leaving behind them horrible dispraise!"

I then: "Master! him fain would I behold
Whelm'd in these dregs, before we quit the lake."

He thus: "Or ever to thy view the shore

Be offer'd, satisfied shall be that wish,
Which well deserves completion." Scarce his words
Were ended, when I saw the miry tribes
Set on him with such violence, that yet
For that render I thanks to God and praise
"To Filippo Argenti:" cried they all:
And on himself the moody Florentine
Turn'd his avenging fangs. Him here we left,
Nor speak I of him more. But on mine ear
Sudden a sound of lamentation smote,
Whereat mine eye unbarr'd I sent abroad.

And thus the good instructor: "Now, my son!
Draws near the city, that of Dis is nam'd,
With its grave denizens, a mighty throng."

I thus: "The minarets already, Sir!
There certes in the valley I descry,
Gleaming vermilion, as if they from fire
Had issu'd." He replied: "Eternal fire,
That inward burns, shows them with ruddy flame
Illum'd; as in this nether hell thou seest."

We came within the fosses deep, that moat
This region comfortless. The walls appear'd
As they were fram'd of iron. We had made
Wide circuit, ere a place we reach'd, where loud
The mariner cried vehement: "Go forth!
The entrance is here!" Upon the gates I spied
More than a thousand, who of old from heaven
Were hurl'd. With ireful gestures, "Who is this,"
They cried, "that without death first felt, goes through
The regions of the dead?" My sapient guide
Made sign that he for secret parley wish'd;
Whereat their angry scorn abating, thus
They spake: "Come thou alone; and let him go
Who hath so hardily enter'd this realm.
Alone return he by his witless way;
If well he know it, let him prove. For thee,
Here shalt thou tarry, who through clime so dark
Hast been his escort." Now bethink thee, reader!
What cheer was mine at sound of those curs'd words.
I did believe I never should return.

"O my lov'd guide! who more than seven times
Security hast render'd me, and drawn
From peril deep, whereto I stood expos'd,
Desert me not," I cried, "in this extreme.
And if our onward going be denied,
Together trace we back our steps with speed."

My liege, who thither had conducted me,
Replied: "Fear not: for of our passage none
Hath power to disappoint us, by such high
Authority permitted. But do thou
Expect me here; meanwhile thy wearied spirit
Comfort, and feed with kindly hope, assur'd
I will not leave thee in this lower world."

This said, departs the sire benevolent,
And quits me. Hesitating I remain
At war 'twixt will and will not in my thoughts.

I could not hear what terms he offer'd them,
But they conferr'd not long, for all at once

To trial fled within. Clos'd were the gates
By those our adversaries on the breast
Of my liege lord: excluded he return'd
To me with tardy steps. Upon the ground
His eyes were bent, and from his brow eras'd
All confidence, while thus with sighs he spake:
"Who hath denied me these abodes of woe?"
Then thus to me: "That I am anger'd, think
No ground of terror: in this trial I
Shall vanquish, use what arts they may within
For hindrance. This their insolence, not new,
Erewhile at gate less secret they display'd,
Which still is without bolt; upon its arch
Thou saw'st the deadly scroll: and even now
On this side of its entrance, down the steep,
Passing the circles, unescorted, comes
One whose strong might can open us this land."

CANTO IX

    The hue, which coward dread on my pale cheeks
Imprinted, when I saw my guide turn back,
Chas'd that from his which newly they had worn,
And inwardly restrain'd it. He, as one
Who listens, stood attentive: for his eye
Not far could lead him through the sable air,
And the thick-gath'ring cloud. "It yet behooves
We win this fight"—thus he began—"if not—
Such aid to us is offer'd.—Oh, how long
Me seems it, ere the promis'd help arrive!"

I noted, how the sequel of his words
Clok'd their beginning; for the last he spake
Agreed not with the first. But not the less
My fear was at his saying; sith I drew
To import worse perchance, than that he held,
His mutilated speech. "Doth ever any
Into this rueful concave's extreme depth
Descend, out of the first degree, whose pain
Is deprivation merely of sweet hope?"

Thus I inquiring. "Rarely," he replied,
"It chances, that among us any makes
This journey, which I wend. Erewhile 'tis true
Once came I here beneath, conjur'd by fell
Erictho, sorceress, who compell'd the shades
Back to their bodies. No long space my flesh
Was naked of me, when within these walls
She made me enter, to draw forth a spirit
From out of Judas' circle. Lowest place
Is that of all, obscurest, and remov'd
Farthest from heav'n's all-circling orb. The road
Full well I know: thou therefore rest secure.
That lake, the noisome stench exhaling, round
The city' of grief encompasses, which now
We may not enter without rage." Yet more
He added: but I hold it not in mind,
For that mine eye toward the lofty tower
Had drawn me wholly, to its burning top.
Where in an instant I beheld uprisen
At once three hellish furies stain'd with blood:

In limb and motion feminine they seem'd;
Around them greenest hydras twisting roll'd
Their volumes; adders and cerastes crept
Instead of hair, and their fierce temples bound.

He knowing well the miserable hags
Who tend the queen of endless woe, thus spake:

    "Mark thou each dire Erinnys. To the left
This is Megaera; on the right hand she,
Who wails, Alecto; and Tisiphone
I' th' midst." This said, in silence he remain'd
Their breast they each one clawing tore; themselves
Smote with their palms, and such shrill clamour rais'd,
That to the bard I clung, suspicion-bound.
"Hasten Medusa: so to adamant

Him shall we change;" all looking down exclaim'd.
"E'en when by Theseus' might assail'd, we took
No ill revenge." "Turn thyself round, and keep
Thy count'nance hid; for if the Gorgon dire
Be shown, and thou shouldst view it, thy return
Upwards would be for ever lost." This said,
Himself my gentle master turn'd me round,
Nor trusted he my hands, but with his own
He also hid me. Ye of intellect
Sound and entire, mark well the lore conceal'd
Under close texture of the mystic strain!

And now there came o'er the perturbed waves
Loud-crashing, terrible, a sound that made
Either shore tremble, as if of a wind
Impetuous, from conflicting vapours sprung,
That 'gainst some forest driving all its might,
Plucks off the branches, beats them down and hurls
Afar; then onward passing proudly sweeps
Its whirlwind rage, while beasts and shepherds fly.

Mine eyes he loos'd, and spake: "And now direct
Thy visual nerve along that ancient foam,
There, thickest where the smoke ascends." As frogs
Before their foe the serpent, through the wave
Ply swiftly all, till at the ground each one
Lies on a heap; more than a thousand spirits
Destroy'd, so saw I fleeing before one
Who pass'd with unwet feet the Stygian sound.
He, from his face removing the gross air,
Oft his left hand forth stretch'd, and seem'd alone
By that annoyance wearied. I perceiv'd
That he was sent from heav'n, and to my guide
Turn'd me, who signal made that I should stand
Quiet, and bend to him. Ah me! how full
Of noble anger seem'd he! To the gate
He came, and with his wand touch'd it, whereat
Open without impediment it flew.

"Outcasts of heav'n! O abject race and scorn'd!"
Began he on the horrid grunsel standing,
"Whence doth this wild excess of insolence
Lodge in you? wherefore kick you 'gainst that will
Ne'er frustrate of its end, and which so oft
Hath laid on you enforcement of your pangs?
What profits at the fays to but the horn?
Your Cerberus, if ye remember, hence
Bears still, peel'd of their hair, his throat and maw."

This said, he turn'd back o'er the filthy way,
And syllable to us spake none, but wore
The semblance of a man by other care
Beset, and keenly press'd, than thought of him
Who in his presence stands. Then we our steps
Toward that territory mov'd, secure
After the hallow'd words. We unoppos'd
There enter'd; and my mind eager to learn
What state a fortress like to that might hold,
I soon as enter'd throw mine eye around,
And see on every part wide-stretching space
Replete with bitter pain and torment ill.

As where Rhone stagnates on the plains of Arles,
Or as at Pola, near Quarnaro's gulf,
That closes Italy and laves her bounds,
The place is all thick spread with sepulchres;
So was it here, save what in horror here
Excell'd: for 'midst the graves were scattered flames,
Wherewith intensely all throughout they burn'd,
That iron for no craft there hotter needs.

Their lids all hung suspended, and beneath
From them forth issu'd lamentable moans,
Such as the sad and tortur'd well might raise.

I thus: "Master! say who are these, interr'd
Within these vaults, of whom distinct we hear
The dolorous sighs?" He answer thus return'd:

"The arch-heretics are here, accompanied
By every sect their followers; and much more,
Than thou believest, tombs are freighted: like
With like is buried; and the monuments
Are different in degrees of heat." This said,
He to the right hand turning, on we pass'd
Betwixt the afflicted and the ramparts high.

CANTO X

    Now by a secret pathway we proceed,
Between the walls, that hem the region round,
And the tormented souls: my master first,
I close behind his steps. "Virtue supreme!"
I thus began; "who through these ample orbs
In circuit lead'st me, even as thou will'st,
Speak thou, and satisfy my wish. May those,
Who lie within these sepulchres, be seen?
Already all the lids are rais'd, and none
O'er them keeps watch." He thus in answer spake
"They shall be closed all, what-time they here
From Josaphat return'd shall come, and bring
Their bodies, which above they now have left.
The cemetery on this part obtain
With Epicurus all his followers,
Who with the body make the spirit die.
Here therefore satisfaction shall be soon
Both to the question ask'd, and to the wish,
Which thou conceal'st in silence." I replied:
"I keep not, guide belov'd! from thee my heart
Secreted, but to shun vain length of words,
A lesson erewhile taught me by thyself."

    "O Tuscan! thou who through the city of fire
Alive art passing, so discreet of speech!
Here please thee stay awhile. Thy utterance
Declares the place of thy nativity
To be that noble land, with which perchance
I too severely dealt." Sudden that sound
Forth issu'd from a vault, whereat in fear
I somewhat closer to my leader's side
Approaching, he thus spake: "What dost thou? Turn.
Lo, Farinata, there! who hath himself
Uplifted: from his girdle upwards all
Expos'd behold him." On his face was mine
Already fix'd; his breast and forehead there
Erecting, seem'd as in high scorn he held
E'en hell. Between the sepulchres to him
My guide thrust me with fearless hands and prompt,
This warning added: "See thy words be clear!"

- 56 -

> He, soon as there I stood at the tomb's foot,
> Ey'd me a space; then in disdainful mood
> Address'd me: "Say, what ancestors were thine."
> Canto X, lines 40–42.

He, soon as there I stood at the tomb's foot,
Ey'd me a space, then in disdainful mood
Address'd me: "Say, what ancestors were thine?"

I, willing to obey him, straight reveal'd
The whole, nor kept back aught: whence he, his brow
Somewhat uplifting, cried: "Fiercely were they
Adverse to me, my party, and the blood
From whence I sprang: twice therefore I abroad
Scatter'd them." "Though driv'n out, yet they each time
From all parts," answer'd I, "return'd; an art
Which yours have shown, they are not skill'd to learn."

Then, peering forth from the unclosed jaw,

Rose from his side a shade, high as the chin,
Leaning, methought, upon its knees uprais'd.
It look'd around, as eager to explore
If there were other with me; but perceiving
That fond imagination quench'd, with tears
Thus spake: "If thou through this blind prison go'st.
Led by thy lofty genius and profound,
Where is my son? and wherefore not with thee?"

I straight replied: "Not of myself I come,
By him, who there expects me, through this clime
Conducted, whom perchance Guido thy son
Had in contempt." Already had his words
And mode of punishment read me his name,
Whence I so fully answer'd. He at once
Exclaim'd, up starting, "How! said'st thou he HAD?
No longer lives he? Strikes not on his eye
The blessed daylight?" Then of some delay
I made ere my reply aware, down fell
Supine, not after forth appear'd he more.

Meanwhile the other, great of soul, near whom
I yet was station'd, chang'd not count'nance stern,
Nor mov'd the neck, nor bent his ribbed side.
"And if," continuing the first discourse,
"They in this art," he cried, "small skill have shown,
That doth torment me more e'en than this bed.
But not yet fifty times shall be relum'd
Her aspect, who reigns here Queen of this realm,
Ere thou shalt know the full weight of that art.
So to the pleasant world mayst thou return,
As thou shalt tell me, why in all their laws,
Against my kin this people is so fell?"

"The slaughter and great havoc," I replied,
"That colour'd Arbia's flood with crimson stain—
To these impute, that in our hallow'd dome
Such orisons ascend." Sighing he shook
The head, then thus resum'd: "In that affray
I stood not singly, nor without just cause
Assuredly should with the rest have stirr'd;
But singly there I stood, when by consent
Of all, Florence had to the ground been raz'd,

The one who openly forbad the deed."

"So may thy lineage find at last repose,"
I thus adjur'd him, "as thou solve this knot,
Which now involves my mind. If right I hear,
Ye seem to view beforehand, that which time
Leads with him, of the present uninform'd."

"We view, as one who hath an evil sight,"
He answer'd, "plainly, objects far remote:
So much of his large spendour yet imparts
The Almighty Ruler; but when they approach
Or actually exist, our intellect
Then wholly fails, nor of your human state
Except what others bring us know we aught.
Hence therefore mayst thou understand, that all
Our knowledge in that instant shall expire,
When on futurity the portals close."

Then conscious of my fault, and by remorse
Smitten, I added thus: "Now shalt thou say
To him there fallen, that his offspring still
Is to the living join'd; and bid him know,
That if from answer silent I abstain'd,
'Twas that my thought was occupied intent
Upon that error, which thy help hath solv'd."

But now my master summoning me back
I heard, and with more eager haste besought
The spirit to inform me, who with him
Partook his lot. He answer thus return'd:

"More than a thousand with me here are laid
Within is Frederick, second of that name,
And the Lord Cardinal, and of the rest
I speak not." He, this said, from sight withdrew.
But I my steps towards the ancient bard
Reverting, ruminated on the words
Betokening me such ill. Onward he mov'd,
And thus in going question'd: "Whence the amaze
That holds thy senses wrapt?" I satisfied
The inquiry, and the sage enjoin'd me straight:
"Let thy safe memory store what thou hast heard

To thee importing harm; and note thou this,"
With his rais'd finger bidding me take heed,

"When thou shalt stand before her gracious beam,
Whose bright eye all surveys, she of thy life
The future tenour will to thee unfold."

Forthwith he to the left hand turn'd his feet:
We left the wall, and tow'rds the middle space
Went by a path, that to a valley strikes;
Which e'en thus high exhal'd its noisome steam.

CANTO XI

Upon the utmost verge of a high bank,
By craggy rocks environ'd round, we came,
Where woes beneath more cruel yet were stow'd:
And here to shun the horrible excess
Of fetid exhalation, upward cast
From the profound abyss, behind the lid
Of a great monument we stood retir'd,

Whereon this scroll I mark'd: "I have in charge
Pope Anastasius, whom Photinus drew
From the right path.—Ere our descent behooves
We make delay, that somewhat first the sense,
To the dire breath accustom'd, afterward

Regard it not." My master thus; to whom
Answering I spake: "Some compensation find
That the time past not wholly lost." He then:
"Lo! how my thoughts e'en to thy wishes tend!
My son! within these rocks," he thus began,
"Are three close circles in gradation plac'd,
As these which now thou leav'st. Each one is full
Of spirits accurs'd; but that the sight alone
Hereafter may suffice thee, listen how
And for what cause in durance they abide.

"Of all malicious act abhorr'd in heaven,
The end is injury; and all such end
Either by force or fraud works other's woe
But fraud, because of man peculiar evil,
To God is more displeasing; and beneath
The fraudulent are therefore doom'd to' endure
Severer pang. The violent occupy
All the first circle; and because to force
Three persons are obnoxious, in three rounds
Each within other sep'rate is it fram'd.
To God, his neighbour, and himself, by man
Force may be offer'd; to himself I say
And his possessions, as thou soon shalt hear
At full. Death, violent death, and painful wounds
Upon his neighbour he inflicts; and wastes
By devastation, pillage, and the flames,
His substance. Slayers, and each one that smites
In malice, plund'rers, and all robbers, hence
The torment undergo of the first round
In different herds. Man can do violence
To himself and his own blessings: and for this
He in the second round must aye deplore
With unavailing penitence his crime,
Whoe'er deprives himself of life and light,
In reckless lavishment his talent wastes,
And sorrows there where he should dwell in joy.
To God may force be offer'd, in the heart
Denying and blaspheming his high power,
And nature with her kindly law contemning.
And thence the inmost round marks with its seal
Sodom and Cahors, and all such as speak
Contemptuously of the Godhead in their hearts.

"Fraud, that in every conscience leaves a sting,
May be by man employ'd on one, whose trust
He wins, or on another who withholds
Strict confidence. Seems as the latter way
Broke but the bond of love which Nature makes.
Whence in the second circle have their nest
Dissimulation, witchcraft, flatteries,
Theft, falsehood, simony, all who seduce
To lust, or set their honesty at pawn,
With such vile scum as these. The other way
Forgets both Nature's general love, and that
Which thereto added afterwards gives birth
To special faith. Whence in the lesser circle,
Point of the universe, dread seat of Dis,
The traitor is eternally consum'd."

I thus: "Instructor, clearly thy discourse
Proceeds, distinguishing the hideous chasm
And its inhabitants with skill exact.
But tell me this: they of the dull, fat pool,
Whom the rain beats, or whom the tempest drives,
Or who with tongues so fierce conflicting meet,
Wherefore within the city fire-illum'd
Are not these punish'd, if God's wrath be on them?
And if it be not, wherefore in such guise
Are they condemned?" He answer thus return'd:
"Wherefore in dotage wanders thus thy mind,
Not so accustom'd? or what other thoughts
Possess it? Dwell not in thy memory
The words, wherein thy ethic page describes
Three dispositions adverse to Heav'n's will,
Incont'nence, malice, and mad brutishness,
And how incontinence the least offends
God, and least guilt incurs? If well thou note
This judgment, and remember who they are,
Without these walls to vain repentance doom'd,
Thou shalt discern why they apart are plac'd
From these fell spirits, and less wreakful pours
Justice divine on them its vengeance down."

"O Sun! who healest all imperfect sight,
Thou so content'st me, when thou solv'st my doubt,

That ignorance not less than knowledge charms.
Yet somewhat turn thee back," I in these words
Continu'd, "where thou saidst, that usury
Offends celestial Goodness; and this knot
Perplex'd unravel." He thus made reply:
"Philosophy, to an attentive ear,
Clearly points out, not in one part alone,
How imitative nature takes her course
From the celestial mind and from its art:
And where her laws the Stagyrite unfolds,
Not many leaves scann'd o'er, observing well
Thou shalt discover, that your art on her
Obsequious follows, as the learner treads
In his instructor's step, so that your art
Deserves the name of second in descent
From God. These two, if thou recall to mind
Creation's holy book, from the beginning
Were the right source of life and excellence
To human kind. But in another path
The usurer walks; and Nature in herself
And in her follower thus he sets at nought,
Placing elsewhere his hope. But follow now
My steps on forward journey bent; for now
The Pisces play with undulating glance
Along the horizon, and the Wain lies all
O'er the north-west; and onward there a space
Is our steep passage down the rocky height."

CANTO XII

    The place where to descend the precipice
We came, was rough as Alp, and on its verge
Such object lay, as every eye would shun.

As is that ruin, which Adice's stream
On this side Trento struck, should'ring the wave,
Or loos'd by earthquake or for lack of prop;
For from the mountain's summit, whence it mov'd
To the low level, so the headlong rock
Is shiver'd, that some passage it might give
To him who from above would pass; e'en such
Into the chasm was that descent: and there
At point of the disparted ridge lay stretch'd
The infamy of Crete, detested brood
Of the feign'd heifer: and at sight of us
It gnaw'd itself, as one with rage distract.

And there
At point of the departed ridge lay stretch'd
The infamy of Crete, detested brood
Of the feign'd heifer.
Canto XII, lines 11-14

    To him my guide exclaim'd: "Perchance thou deem'st
The King of Athens here, who, in the world
Above, thy death contriv'd. Monster! avaunt!
He comes not tutor'd by thy sister's art,
But to behold your torments is he come."

Like to a bull, that with impetuous spring
Darts, at the moment when the fatal blow
Hath struck him, but unable to proceed
Plunges on either side; so saw I plunge
The Minotaur; whereat the sage exclaim'd:
"Run to the passage! while he storms, 't is well
That thou descend." Thus down our road we took
Through those dilapidated crags, that oft
Mov'd underneath my feet, to weight like theirs

Unus'd. I pond'ring went, and thus he spake:

"Perhaps thy thoughts are of this ruin'd steep,
Guarded by the brute violence, which I
Have vanquish'd now. Know then, that when I erst
Hither descended to the nether hell,
This rock was not yet fallen. But past doubt
(If well I mark) not long ere He arrived,
Who carried off from Dis the mighty spoil
Of the highest circle, then through all its bounds
Such trembling seiz'd the deep concave and foul,
I thought the universe was thrill'd with love,
Whereby, there are who deem, the world hath oft
Been into chaos turn'd: and in that point,
Here, and elsewhere, that old rock toppled down.
But fix thine eyes beneath: the river of blood
Approaches, in the which all those are steep'd,
Who have by violence injur'd." O blind lust!
O foolish wrath! who so dost goad us on
In the brief life, and in the eternal then
Thus miserably o'erwhelm us. I beheld
An ample foss, that in a bow was bent,
As circling all the plain; for so my guide
Had told. Between it and the rampart's base
On trail ran Centaurs, with keen arrows arm'd,
As to the chase they on the earth were wont.

*One cried from far : "Say, to what pain ye come
Condemn'd, who down this steep have journied."
Canto XII., lines 58, 59.*

    At seeing us descend they each one stood;
And issuing from the troop, three sped with bows
And missile weapons chosen first; of whom
One cried from far: "Say to what pain ye come
Condemn'd, who down this steep have journied? Speak
From whence ye stand, or else the bow I draw."

To whom my guide: "Our answer shall be made
To Chiron, there, when nearer him we come.
Ill was thy mind, thus ever quick and rash."

Then me he touch'd, and spake: "Nessus is this,
Who for the fair Deianira died,
And wrought himself revenge for his own fate.
He in the midst, that on his breast looks down,
Is the great Chiron who Achilles nurs'd;
That other Pholus, prone to wrath." Around
The foss these go by thousands, aiming shafts
At whatsoever spirit dares emerge
From out the blood, more than his guilt allows.

We to those beasts, that rapid strode along,
Drew near, when Chiron took an arrow forth,
And with the notch push'd back his shaggy beard
To the cheek-bone, then his great mouth to view
Exposing, to his fellows thus exclaim'd:
"Are ye aware, that he who comes behind
Moves what he touches? The feet of the dead
Are not so wont." My trusty guide, who now
Stood near his breast, where the two natures join,
Thus made reply: "He is indeed alive,
And solitary so must needs by me
Be shown the gloomy vale, thereto induc'd
By strict necessity, not by delight.
She left her joyful harpings in the sky,
Who this new office to my care consign'd.
He is no robber, no dark spirit I.
But by that virtue, which empowers my step
To treat so wild a path, grant us, I pray,
One of thy band, whom we may trust secure,
Who to the ford may lead us, and convey
Across, him mounted on his back; for he
Is not a spirit that may walk the air."

Then on his right breast turning, Chiron thus
To Nessus spake: "Return, and be their guide.
And if ye chance to cross another troop,
Command them keep aloof." Onward we mov'd,
The faithful escort by our side, along
The border of the crimson-seething flood,
Whence from those steep'd within loud shrieks arose.

Some there I mark'd, as high as to their brow
Immers'd, of whom the mighty Centaur thus:
"These are the souls of tyrants, who were given
To blood and rapine. Here they wail aloud
Their merciless wrongs. Here Alexander dwells,
And Dionysius fell, who many a year
Of woe wrought for fair Sicily. That brow
Whereon the hair so jetty clust'ring hangs,
Is Azzolino; that with flaxen locks
Obizzo' of Este, in the world destroy'd
By his foul step-son." To the bard rever'd
I turned me round, and thus he spake; "Let him
Be to thee now first leader, me but next
To him in rank." Then farther on a space
The Centaur paus'd, near some, who at the throat
Were extant from the wave; and showing us
A spirit by itself apart retir'd,
Exclaim'd: "He in God's bosom smote the heart,
Which yet is honour'd on the bank of Thames."

A race I next espied, who held the head,
And even all the bust above the stream.
'Midst these I many a face remember'd well.
Thus shallow more and more the blood became,
So that at last it but imbru'd the feet;
And there our passage lay athwart the foss.

"As ever on this side the boiling wave
Thou seest diminishing," the Centaur said,
"So on the other, be thou well assur'd,
It lower still and lower sinks its bed,
Till in that part it reuniting join,
Where 't is the lot of tyranny to mourn.
There Heav'n's stern justice lays chastising hand
On Attila, who was the scourge of earth,

On Sextus, and on Pyrrhus, and extracts
Tears ever by the seething flood unlock'd
From the Rinieri, of Corneto this,
Pazzo the other nam'd, who fill'd the ways
With violence and war." This said, he turn'd,
And quitting us, alone repass'd the ford.

CANTO XIII

    Ere Nessus yet had reach'd the other bank,
We enter'd on a forest, where no track
Of steps had worn a way. Not verdant there
The foliage, but of dusky hue; not light
The boughs and tapering, but with knares deform'd
And matted thick: fruits there were none, but thorns
Instead, with venom fill'd. Less sharp than these,
Less intricate the brakes, wherein abide
Those animals, that hate the cultur'd fields,
Betwixt Corneto and Cecina's stream.

Here the brute Harpies make their nest.
Canto XIII., line 12.

    Here the brute Harpies make their nest, the same
Who from the Strophades the Trojan band
Drove with dire boding of their future woe.

Broad are their pennons, of the human form
Their neck and count'nance, arm'd with talons keen
The feet, and the huge belly fledge with wings
These sit and wail on the drear mystic wood.

The kind instructor in these words began:
"Ere farther thou proceed, know thou art now
I' th' second round, and shalt be, till thou come
Upon the horrid sand: look therefore well
Around thee, and such things thou shalt behold,
As would my speech discredit." On all sides
I heard sad plainings breathe, and none could see
From whom they might have issu'd. In amaze
Fast bound I stood. He, as it seem'd, believ'd,
That I had thought so many voices came
From some amid those thickets close conceal'd,
And thus his speech resum'd: "If thou lop off
A single twig from one of those ill plants,
The thought thou hast conceiv'd shall vanish quite."

Thereat a little stretching forth my hand,
From a great wilding gather'd I a branch,
And straight the trunk exclaim'd: "Why pluck'st thou me?"

And straight the trunk exclaim'd, "Why pluck'st thou me?"
Canto XIII. line 34.

Then as the dark blood trickled down its side,
These words it added: "Wherefore tear'st me thus?
Is there no touch of mercy in thy breast?
Men once were we, that now are rooted here.
Thy hand might well have spar'd us, had we been
The souls of serpents." As a brand yet green,
That burning at one end from the other sends
A groaning sound, and hisses with the wind
That forces out its way, so burst at once,
Forth from the broken splinter words and blood.

I, letting fall the bough, remain'd as one
Assail'd by terror, and the sage replied:
"If he, O injur'd spirit! could have believ'd
What he hath seen but in my verse describ'd,
He never against thee had stretch'd his hand.
But I, because the thing surpass'd belief,
Prompted him to this deed, which even now
Myself I rue. But tell me, who thou wast;
That, for this wrong to do thee some amends,
In the upper world (for thither to return
Is granted him) thy fame he may revive."

"That pleasant word of thine," the trunk replied
"Hath so inveigled me, that I from speech
Cannot refrain, wherein if I indulge
A little longer, in the snare detain'd,
Count it not grievous. I it was, who held
Both keys to Frederick's heart, and turn'd the wards,
Opening and shutting, with a skill so sweet,
That besides me, into his inmost breast
Scarce any other could admittance find.
The faith I bore to my high charge was such,
It cost me the life-blood that warm'd my veins.
The harlot, who ne'er turn'd her gloating eyes
From Caesar's household, common vice and pest
Of courts, 'gainst me inflam'd the minds of all;
And to Augustus they so spread the flame,
That my glad honours chang'd to bitter woes.
My soul, disdainful and disgusted, sought
Refuge in death from scorn, and I became,
Just as I was, unjust toward myself.
By the new roots, which fix this stem, I swear,

That never faith I broke to my liege lord,
Who merited such honour; and of you,
If any to the world indeed return,
Clear he from wrong my memory, that lies
Yet prostrate under envy's cruel blow."

First somewhat pausing, till the mournful words
Were ended, then to me the bard began:
"Lose not the time; but speak and of him ask,
If more thou wish to learn." Whence I replied:
"Question thou him again of whatsoe'er
Will, as thou think'st, content me; for no power
Have I to ask, such pity' is at my heart."

He thus resum'd; "So may he do for thee
Freely what thou entreatest, as thou yet
Be pleas'd, imprison'd Spirit! to declare,
How in these gnarled joints the soul is tied;
And whether any ever from such frame
Be loosen'd, if thou canst, that also tell."

Thereat the trunk breath'd hard, and the wind soon
Chang'd into sounds articulate like these;

Briefly ye shall be answer'd. "When departs
The fierce soul from the body, by itself
Thence torn asunder, to the seventh gulf
By Minos doom'd, into the wood it falls,
No place assign'd, but wheresoever chance
Hurls it, there sprouting, as a grain of spelt,
It rises to a sapling, growing thence
A savage plant. The Harpies, on its leaves
Then feeding, cause both pain and for the pain
A vent to grief. We, as the rest, shall come
For our own spoils, yet not so that with them
We may again be clad; for what a man
Takes from himself it is not just he have.
Here we perforce shall drag them; and throughout
The dismal glade our bodies shall be hung,
Each on the wild thorn of his wretched shade."

Attentive yet to listen to the trunk
We stood, expecting farther speech, when us

A noise surpris'd, as when a man perceives
The wild boar and the hunt approach his place
Of station'd watch, who of the beasts and boughs
Loud rustling round him hears. And lo! there came
Two naked, torn with briers, in headlong flight,
That they before them broke each fan o' th' wood.
"Haste now," the foremost cried, "now haste thee death!"

"Haste now," the foremost cried, "now haste thee, death!"
Canto XIII., line 120.

    The other, as seem'd, impatient of delay
Exclaiming, "Lano! not so bent for speed
Thy sinews, in the lists of Toppo's field."
And then, for that perchance no longer breath
Suffic'd him, of himself and of a bush
One group he made. Behind them was the wood
Full of black female mastiffs, gaunt and fleet,
As greyhounds that have newly slipp'd the leash.
On him, who squatted down, they stuck their fangs,
And having rent him piecemeal bore away
The tortur'd limbs. My guide then seiz'd my hand,
And led me to the thicket, which in vain
Mourn'd through its bleeding wounds: "O Giacomo
Of Sant' Andrea! what avails it thee,"

It cried, "that of me thou hast made thy screen?
For thy ill life what blame on me recoils?"

When o'er it he had paus'd, my master spake:
"Say who wast thou, that at so many points
Breath'st out with blood thy lamentable speech?"

He answer'd: "Oh, ye spirits: arriv'd in time
To spy the shameful havoc, that from me
My leaves hath sever'd thus, gather them up,
And at the foot of their sad parent-tree
Carefully lay them. In that city' I dwelt,
Who for the Baptist her first patron chang'd,
Whence he for this shall cease not with his art
To work her woe: and if there still remain'd not
On Arno's passage some faint glimpse of him,
Those citizens, who rear'd once more her walls
Upon the ashes left by Attila,
Had labour'd without profit of their toil.
I slung the fatal noose from my own roof."

CANTO XIV

    Soon as the charity of native land
Wrought in my bosom, I the scatter'd leaves
Collected, and to him restor'd, who now
Was hoarse with utt'rance. To the limit thence
We came, which from the third the second round
Divides, and where of justice is display'd
Contrivance horrible. Things then first seen
Clearlier to manifest, I tell how next
A plain we reach'd, that from its sterile bed
Each plant repell'd. The mournful wood waves round
Its garland on all sides, as round the wood
Spreads the sad foss. There, on the very edge,
Our steps we stay'd. It was an area wide
Of arid sand and thick, resembling most
The soil that erst by Cato's foot was trod.

Vengeance of Heav'n! Oh! how shouldst thou be fear'd
By all, who read what here my eyes beheld!

Of naked spirits many a flock I saw,
All weeping piteously, to different laws
Subjected: for on the earth some lay supine,
Some crouching close were seated, others pac'd
Incessantly around; the latter tribe,
More numerous, those fewer who beneath
The torment lay, but louder in their grief.

O'er all the sand fell slowly wafting down
Dilated flakes of fire, as flakes of snow
On Alpine summit, when the wind is hush'd.
As in the torrid Indian clime, the son
Of Ammon saw upon his warrior band
Descending, solid flames, that to the ground
Came down: whence he bethought him with his troop
To trample on the soil; for easier thus
The vapour was extinguish'd, while alone;
So fell the eternal fiery flood, wherewith
The marble glow'd underneath, as under stove
The viands, doubly to augment the pain.

*Unceasing was the play of wretched hands,
Now this, now that way glancing, to shake off
The heat, still falling fresh.*
                              Canto XIV., lines 37—39.

    Unceasing was the play of wretched hands,
Now this, now that way glancing, to shake off
The heat, still falling fresh. I thus began:
"Instructor! thou who all things overcom'st,
Except the hardy demons, that rush'd forth
To stop our entrance at the gate, say who
Is yon huge spirit, that, as seems, heeds not
The burning, but lies writhen in proud scorn,
As by the sultry tempest immatur'd?"

Straight he himself, who was aware I ask'd
My guide of him, exclaim'd: "Such as I was
When living, dead such now I am. If Jove
Weary his workman out, from whom in ire
He snatch'd the lightnings, that at my last day
Transfix'd me, if the rest be weary out
At their black smithy labouring by turns
In Mongibello, while he cries aloud;
"Help, help, good Mulciber!" as erst he cried
In the Phlegraean warfare, and the bolts

Launch he full aim'd at me with all his might,
He never should enjoy a sweet revenge."

Then thus my guide, in accent higher rais'd
Than I before had heard him: "Capaneus!
Thou art more punish'd, in that this thy pride
Lives yet unquench'd: no torrent, save thy rage,
Were to thy fury pain proportion'd full."

Next turning round to me with milder lip
He spake: "This of the seven kings was one,
Who girt the Theban walls with siege, and held,
As still he seems to hold, God in disdain,
And sets his high omnipotence at nought.
But, as I told him, his despiteful mood
Is ornament well suits the breast that wears it.
Follow me now; and look thou set not yet
Thy foot in the hot sand, but to the wood
Keep ever close." Silently on we pass'd
To where there gushes from the forest's bound
A little brook, whose crimson'd wave yet lifts
My hair with horror. As the rill, that runs
From Bulicame, to be portion'd out
Among the sinful women; so ran this
Down through the sand, its bottom and each bank
Stone-built, and either margin at its side,
Whereon I straight perceiv'd our passage lay.

"Of all that I have shown thee, since that gate
We enter'd first, whose threshold is to none
Denied, nought else so worthy of regard,
As is this river, has thine eye discern'd,
O'er which the flaming volley all is quench'd."

So spake my guide; and I him thence besought,
That having giv'n me appetite to know,
The food he too would give, that hunger crav'd.

"In midst of ocean," forthwith he began,
"A desolate country lies, which Crete is nam'd,
Under whose monarch in old times the world
Liv'd pure and chaste. A mountain rises there,
Call'd Ida, joyous once with leaves and streams,

Deserted now like a forbidden thing.
It was the spot which Rhea, Saturn's spouse,
Chose for the secret cradle of her son;
And better to conceal him, drown'd in shouts
His infant cries. Within the mount, upright
An ancient form there stands and huge, that turns
His shoulders towards Damiata, and at Rome
As in his mirror looks. Of finest gold
His head is shap'd, pure silver are the breast
And arms; thence to the middle is of brass.
And downward all beneath well-temper'd steel,
Save the right foot of potter's clay, on which
Than on the other more erect he stands,
Each part except the gold, is rent throughout;
And from the fissure tears distil, which join'd
Penetrate to that cave. They in their course
Thus far precipitated down the rock
Form Acheron, and Styx, and Phlegethon;
Then by this straiten'd channel passing hence
Beneath, e'en to the lowest depth of all,
Form there Cocytus, of whose lake (thyself
Shall see it) I here give thee no account."

Then I to him: "If from our world this sluice
Be thus deriv'd; wherefore to us but now
Appears it at this edge?" He straight replied:
"The place, thou know'st, is round; and though great part
Thou have already pass'd, still to the left
Descending to the nethermost, not yet
Hast thou the circuit made of the whole orb.
Wherefore if aught of new to us appear,
It needs not bring up wonder in thy looks."

Then I again inquir'd: "Where flow the streams
Of Phlegethon and Lethe? for of one
Thou tell'st not, and the other of that shower,
Thou say'st, is form'd." He answer thus return'd:
"Doubtless thy questions all well pleas'd I hear.
Yet the red seething wave might have resolv'd
One thou proposest. Lethe thou shalt see,
But not within this hollow, in the place,
Whither to lave themselves the spirits go,
Whose blame hath been by penitence remov'd."

He added: "Time is now we quit the wood.
Look thou my steps pursue: the margins give
Safe passage, unimpeded by the flames;
For over them all vapour is extinct."

CANTO XV

One of the solid margins bears us now
Envelop'd in the mist, that from the stream
Arising, hovers o'er, and saves from fire
Both piers and water. As the Flemings rear
Their mound, 'twixt Ghent and Bruges, to chase back
The ocean, fearing his tumultuous tide
That drives toward them, or the Paduans theirs
Along the Brenta, to defend their towns
And castles, ere the genial warmth be felt
On Chiarentana's top; such were the mounds,
So fram'd, though not in height or bulk to these
Made equal, by the master, whosoe'er
He was, that rais'd them here. We from the wood
Were not so far remov'd, that turning round
I might not have discern'd it, when we met
A troop of spirits, who came beside the pier.

They each one ey'd us, as at eventide
One eyes another under a new moon,
And toward us sharpen'd their sight as keen,
As an old tailor at his needle's eye.

Thus narrowly explor'd by all the tribe,
I was agniz'd of one, who by the skirt
Caught me, and cried, "What wonder have we here!"

And I, when he to me outstretch'd his arm,
Intently fix'd my ken on his parch'd looks,
That although smirch'd with fire, they hinder'd not
But I remember'd him; and towards his face
My hand inclining, answer'd: "Sir! Brunetto!

"And art thou here?" He thus to me: "My son!
Oh let it not displease thee, if Brunetto
Latini but a little space with thee
Turn back, and leave his fellows to proceed."

I thus to him replied: "Much as I can,
I thereto pray thee; and if thou be willing,
That I here seat me with thee, I consent;
His leave, with whom I journey, first obtain'd."

"O son!" said he, "whoever of this throng
One instant stops, lies then a hundred years,
No fan to ventilate him, when the fire
Smites sorest. Pass thou therefore on. I close
Will at thy garments walk, and then rejoin
My troop, who go mourning their endless doom."

I dar'd not from the path descend to tread
On equal ground with him, but held my head
Bent down, as one who walks in reverent guise.

"What chance or destiny," thus he began,
"Ere the last day conducts thee here below?
And who is this, that shows to thee the way?"

"There up aloft," I answer'd, "in the life
Serene, I wander'd in a valley lost,
Before mine age had to its fullness reach'd.
But yester-morn I left it: then once more
Into that vale returning, him I met;
And by this path homeward he leads me back."

"If thou," he answer'd, "follow but thy star,
Thou canst not miss at last a glorious haven:
Unless in fairer days my judgment err'd.
And if my fate so early had not chanc'd,
Seeing the heav'ns thus bounteous to thee, I
Had gladly giv'n thee comfort in thy work.
But that ungrateful and malignant race,
Who in old times came down from Fesole,
Ay and still smack of their rough mountain-flint,
Will for thy good deeds shew thee enmity.
Nor wonder; for amongst ill-savour'd crabs
It suits not the sweet fig-tree lay her fruit.
Old fame reports them in the world for blind,
Covetous, envious, proud. Look to it well:
Take heed thou cleanse thee of their ways. For thee
Thy fortune hath such honour in reserve,
That thou by either party shalt be crav'd
With hunger keen: but be the fresh herb far
From the goat's tooth. The herd of Fesole
May of themselves make litter, not touch the plant,
If any such yet spring on their rank bed,
In which the holy seed revives, transmitted
From those true Romans, who still there remain'd,
When it was made the nest of so much ill."

"Were all my wish fulfill'd," I straight replied,
"Thou from the confines of man's nature yet
Hadst not been driven forth; for in my mind
Is fix'd, and now strikes full upon my heart
The dear, benign, paternal image, such
As thine was, when so lately thou didst teach me
The way for man to win eternity;

And how I priz'd the lesson, it behooves,
That, long as life endures, my tongue should speak,
What of my fate thou tell'st, that write I down:
And with another text to comment on
For her I keep it, the celestial dame,
Who will know all, if I to her arrive.
This only would I have thee clearly note:
That so my conscience have no plea against me;
Do fortune as she list, I stand prepar'd.
Not new or strange such earnest to mine ear.
Speed fortune then her wheel, as likes her best,
The clown his mattock; all things have their course."

Thereat my sapient guide upon his right
Turn'd himself back, then look'd at me and spake:
"He listens to good purpose who takes note."

I not the less still on my way proceed,
Discoursing with Brunetto, and inquire
Who are most known and chief among his tribe.

"To know of some is well;" thus he replied,
"But of the rest silence may best beseem.
Time would not serve us for report so long.
In brief I tell thee, that all these were clerks,
Men of great learning and no less renown,
By one same sin polluted in the world.
With them is Priscian, and Accorso's son
Francesco herds among that wretched throng:
And, if the wish of so impure a blotch
Possess'd thee, him thou also might'st have seen,
Who by the servants' servant was transferr'd
From Arno's seat to Bacchiglione, where
His ill-strain'd nerves he left. I more would add,
But must from farther speech and onward way
Alike desist, for yonder I behold
A mist new-risen on the sandy plain.
A company, with whom I may not sort,
Approaches. I commend my TREASURE to thee,
Wherein I yet survive; my sole request."

This said he turn'd, and seem'd as one of those,
Who o'er Verona's champain try their speed

For the green mantle, and of them he seem'd,
Not he who loses but who gains the prize.

CANTO XVI

Now came I where the water's din was heard,
As down it fell into the other round,
Resounding like the hum of swarming bees:
When forth together issu'd from a troop,
That pass'd beneath the fierce tormenting storm,
Three spirits, running swift. They towards us came,
And each one cried aloud, "Oh do thou stay!
Whom by the fashion of thy garb we deem
To be some inmate of our evil land."

Ah me! what wounds I mark'd upon their limbs,
Recent and old, inflicted by the flames!
E'en the remembrance of them grieves me yet.

Attentive to their cry my teacher paus'd,
And turn'd to me his visage, and then spake;
"Wait now! our courtesy these merit well:
And were 't not for the nature of the place,
Whence glide the fiery darts, I should have said,
That haste had better suited thee than them."

They, when we stopp'd, resum'd their ancient wail,
And soon as they had reach'd us, all the three
Whirl'd round together in one restless wheel.
As naked champions, smear'd with slippery oil,
Are wont intent to watch their place of hold
And vantage, ere in closer strife they meet;
Thus each one, as he wheel'd, his countenance
At me directed, so that opposite
The neck mov'd ever to the twinkling feet.

"If misery of this drear wilderness,"
Thus one began, "added to our sad cheer
And destitute, do call forth scorn on us
And our entreaties, let our great renown
Incline thee to inform us who thou art,
That dost imprint with living feet unharm'd
The soil of Hell. He, in whose track thou see'st
My steps pursuing, naked though he be
And reft of all, was of more high estate
Than thou believest; grandchild of the chaste

Gualdrada, him they Guidoguerra call'd,
Who in his lifetime many a noble act
Achiev'd, both by his wisdom and his sword.
The other, next to me that beats the sand,
Is Aldobrandi, name deserving well,
In the upper world, of honour; and myself
Who in this torment do partake with them,
Am Rusticucci, whom, past doubt, my wife
Of savage temper, more than aught beside
Hath to this evil brought." If from the fire
I had been shelter'd, down amidst them straight
I then had cast me, nor my guide, I deem,
Would have restrain'd my going; but that fear
Of the dire burning vanquish'd the desire,
Which made me eager of their wish'd embrace.

I then began: "Not scorn, but grief much more,
Such as long time alone can cure, your doom
Fix'd deep within me, soon as this my lord
Spake words, whose tenour taught me to expect
That such a race, as ye are, was at hand.
I am a countryman of yours, who still
Affectionate have utter'd, and have heard
Your deeds and names renown'd. Leaving the gall
For the sweet fruit I go, that a sure guide
Hath promis'd to me. But behooves, that far
As to the centre first I downward tend."

"So may long space thy spirit guide thy limbs,"
He answer straight return'd; "and so thy fame
Shine bright, when thou art gone; as thou shalt tell,
If courtesy and valour, as they wont,
Dwell in our city, or have vanish'd clean?
For one amidst us late condemn'd to wail,
Borsiere, yonder walking with his peers,
Grieves us no little by the news he brings."

"An upstart multitude and sudden gains,
Pride and excess, O Florence! have in thee
Engender'd, so that now in tears thou mourn'st!"
Thus cried I with my face uprais'd, and they
All three, who for an answer took my words,
Look'd at each other, as men look when truth

Comes to their ear. "If thou at other times,"
They all at once rejoin'd, "so easily
Satisfy those, who question, happy thou,
Gifted with words, so apt to speak thy thought!
Wherefore if thou escape this darksome clime,
Returning to behold the radiant stars,
When thou with pleasure shalt retrace the past,
See that of us thou speak among mankind."

This said, they broke the circle, and so swift
Fled, that as pinions seem'd their nimble feet.

Not in so short a time might one have said
"Amen," as they had vanish'd. Straight my guide
Pursu'd his track. I follow'd; and small space
Had we pass'd onward, when the water's sound
Was now so near at hand, that we had scarce
Heard one another's speech for the loud din.

E'en as the river, that holds on its course
Unmingled, from the mount of Vesulo,
On the left side of Apennine, toward
The east, which Acquacheta higher up
They call, ere it descend into the vale,
At Forli by that name no longer known,
Rebellows o'er Saint Benedict, roll'd on
From the Alpine summit down a precipice,
Where space enough to lodge a thousand spreads;
Thus downward from a craggy steep we found,
That this dark wave resounded, roaring loud,
So that the ear its clamour soon had stunn'd.

I had a cord that brac'd my girdle round,
Wherewith I erst had thought fast bound to take
The painted leopard. This when I had all
Unloosen'd from me (so my master bade)
I gather'd up, and stretch'd it forth to him.
Then to the right he turn'd, and from the brink
Standing few paces distant, cast it down
Into the deep abyss. "And somewhat strange,"
Thus to myself I spake, "signal so strange
Betokens, which my guide with earnest eye
Thus follows." Ah! what caution must men use

With those who look not at the deed alone,
But spy into the thoughts with subtle skill!

"Quickly shall come," he said, "what I expect,
Thine eye discover quickly, that whereof
Thy thought is dreaming." Ever to that truth,
Which but the semblance of a falsehood wears,
A man, if possible, should bar his lip;
Since, although blameless, he incurs reproach.
But silence here were vain; and by these notes
Which now I sing, reader! I swear to thee,
So may they favour find to latest times!
That through the gross and murky air I spied
A shape come swimming up, that might have quell'd
The stoutest heart with wonder, in such guise
As one returns, who hath been down to loose
An anchor grappled fast against some rock,
Or to aught else that in the salt wave lies,
Who upward springing close draws in his feet.

CANTO XVII

"Lo! the fell monster with the deadly sting!
Who passes mountains, breaks through fenced walls
And firm embattled spears, and with his filth
Taints all the world!" Thus me my guide address'd,
And beckon'd him, that he should come to shore,
Near to the stony causeway's utmost edge.

Forthwith that image vile of Fraud appear'd.
Canto XVII, line 7.

Forthwith that image vile of fraud appear'd,
His head and upper part expos'd on land,
But laid not on the shore his bestial train.
His face the semblance of a just man's wore,
So kind and gracious was its outward cheer;
The rest was serpent all: two shaggy claws

- 92 -

Reach'd to the armpits, and the back and breast,
And either side, were painted o'er with nodes
And orbits. Colours variegated more
Nor Turks nor Tartars e'er on cloth of state
With interchangeable embroidery wove,
Nor spread Arachne o'er her curious loom.
As ofttimes a light skiff, moor'd to the shore,
Stands part in water, part upon the land;
Or, as where dwells the greedy German boor,
The beaver settles watching for his prey;
So on the rim, that fenc'd the sand with rock,
Sat perch'd the fiend of evil. In the void
Glancing, his tail upturn'd its venomous fork,
With sting like scorpion's arm'd. Then thus my guide:
"Now need our way must turn few steps apart,
Far as to that ill beast, who couches there."

Thereat toward the right our downward course
We shap'd, and, better to escape the flame
And burning marle, ten paces on the verge
Proceeded. Soon as we to him arrive,
A little further on mine eye beholds
A tribe of spirits, seated on the sand
Near the wide chasm. Forthwith my master spake:
"That to the full thy knowledge may extend
Of all this round contains, go now, and mark
The mien these wear: but hold not long discourse.
Till thou returnest, I with him meantime
Will parley, that to us he may vouchsafe
The aid of his strong shoulders." Thus alone
Yet forward on the extremity I pac'd
Of that seventh circle, where the mournful tribe
Were seated. At the eyes forth gush'd their pangs.
Against the vapours and the torrid soil
Alternately their shifting hands they plied.
Thus use the dogs in summer still to ply
Their jaws and feet by turns, when bitten sore
By gnats, or flies, or gadflies swarming round.

Noting the visages of some, who lay
Beneath the pelting of that dolorous fire,
One of them all I knew not; but perceiv'd,
That pendent from his neck each bore a pouch

With colours and with emblems various mark'd,
On which it seem'd as if their eye did feed.

And when amongst them looking round I came,
A yellow purse I saw with azure wrought,
That wore a lion's countenance and port.
Then still my sight pursuing its career,
Another I beheld, than blood more red.
A goose display of whiter wing than curd.
And one, who bore a fat and azure swine
Pictur'd on his white scrip, addressed me thus:
"What dost thou in this deep? Go now and know,
Since yet thou livest, that my neighbour here
Vitaliano on my left shall sit.
A Paduan with these Florentines am I.
Ofttimes they thunder in mine ears, exclaiming
'O haste that noble knight! he who the pouch
With the three beaks will bring!'" This said, he writh'd
The mouth, and loll'd the tongue out, like an ox
That licks his nostrils. I, lest longer stay
He ill might brook, who bade me stay not long,
Backward my steps from those sad spirits turn'd.

My guide already seated on the haunch
Of the fierce animal I found; and thus
He me encourag'd. "Be thou stout; be bold.
Down such a steep flight must we now descend!
Mount thou before: for that no power the tail
May have to harm thee, I will be i' th' midst."

As one, who hath an ague fit so near,
His nails already are turn'd blue, and he
Quivers all o'er, if he but eye the shade;
Such was my cheer at hearing of his words.
But shame soon interpos'd her threat, who makes
The servant bold in presence of his lord.

I settled me upon those shoulders huge,
And would have said, but that the words to aid
My purpose came not, "Look thou clasp me firm!"

But he whose succour then not first I prov'd,
Soon as I mounted, in his arms aloft,

Embracing, held me up, and thus he spake:
"Geryon! now move thee! be thy wheeling gyres
Of ample circuit, easy thy descent.
Think on th' unusual burden thou sustain'st."

As a small vessel, back'ning out from land,
Her station quits; so thence the monster loos'd,
And when he felt himself at large, turn'd round
There where the breast had been, his forked tail.
Thus, like an eel, outstretch'd at length he steer'd,
Gath'ring the air up with retractile claws.

Not greater was the dread when Phaeton
The reins let drop at random, whence high heaven,
Whereof signs yet appear, was wrapt in flames;
Nor when ill-fated Icarus perceiv'd,
By liquefaction of the scalded wax,
The trusted pennons loosen'd from his loins,
His sire exclaiming loud, "Ill way thou keep'st!"
Than was my dread, when round me on each part
The air I view'd, and other object none
Save the fell beast. He slowly sailing, wheels
His downward motion, unobserv'd of me,
But that the wind, arising to my face,
Breathes on me from below. Now on our right
I heard the cataract beneath us leap
With hideous crash; whence bending down to' explore,
New terror I conceiv'd at the steep plunge:

New terror I conceived at the steep plunge.
Canto XVII. line 117.

    For flames I saw, and wailings smote mine ear:
So that all trembling close I crouch'd my limbs,
And then distinguish'd, unperceiv'd before,
By the dread torments that on every side
Drew nearer, how our downward course we wound.

As falcon, that hath long been on the wing,
But lure nor bird hath seen, while in despair
The falconer cries, "Ah me! thou stoop'st to earth!"
Wearied descends, and swiftly down the sky
In many an orbit wheels, then lighting sits
At distance from his lord in angry mood;
So Geryon lighting places us on foot
Low down at base of the deep-furrow'd rock,
And, of his burden there discharg'd, forthwith
Sprang forward, like an arrow from the string.

CANTO XVIII

There is a place within the depths of hell
Call'd Malebolge, all of rock dark-stain'd
With hue ferruginous, e'en as the steep
That round it circling winds. Right in the midst
Of that abominable region, yawns
A spacious gulf profound, whereof the frame
Due time shall tell. The circle, that remains,
Throughout its round, between the gulf and base
Of the high craggy banks, successive forms
Ten trenches, in its hollow bottom sunk.

As where to guard the walls, full many a foss
Begirds some stately castle, sure defence
Affording to the space within, so here
Were model'd these; and as like fortresses
E'en from their threshold to the brink without,
Are flank'd with bridges; from the rock's low base
Thus flinty paths advanc'd, that 'cross the moles
And dikes, struck onward far as to the gulf,
That in one bound collected cuts them off.
Such was the place, wherein we found ourselves
From Geryon's back dislodg'd. The bard to left
Held on his way, and I behind him mov'd.

On our right hand new misery I saw,
New pains, new executioners of wrath,
That swarming peopled the first chasm. Below
Were naked sinners. Hitherward they came,
Meeting our faces from the middle point,
With us beyond but with a larger stride.
E'en thus the Romans, when the year returns
Of Jubilee, with better speed to rid
The thronging multitudes, their means devise
For such as pass the bridge; that on one side
All front toward the castle, and approach
Saint Peter's fane, on th' other towards the mount.

Each divers way along the grisly rock,
Horn'd demons I beheld, with lashes huge,
That on their back unmercifully smote.
Ah! how they made them bound at the first stripe!

Ah! how they made them bound at the first stripe!
Canto XVIII., line 38.

    None for the second waited nor the third.

Meantime as on I pass'd, one met my sight
Whom soon as view'd; "Of him," cried I, "not yet
Mine eye hath had his fill." With fixed gaze
I therefore scann'd him. Straight the teacher kind
Paus'd with me, and consented I should walk
Backward a space, and the tormented spirit,
Who thought to hide him, bent his visage down.
But it avail'd him nought; for I exclaim'd:
"Thou who dost cast thy eye upon the ground,
Unless thy features do belie thee much,
Venedico art thou. But what brings thee
Into this bitter seas'ning?" He replied:
"Unwillingly I answer to thy words.
But thy clear speech, that to my mind recalls
The world I once inhabited, constrains me.
Know then 'twas I who led fair Ghisola
To do the Marquis' will, however fame
The shameful tale have bruited. Nor alone
Bologna hither sendeth me to mourn
Rather with us the place is so o'erthrong'd
That not so many tongues this day are taught,

Betwixt the Reno and Savena's stream,
To answer SIPA in their country's phrase.
And if of that securer proof thou need,
Remember but our craving thirst for gold."

Him speaking thus, a demon with his thong
Struck, and exclaim'd, "Away! corrupter! here
Women are none for sale." Forthwith I join'd
My escort, and few paces thence we came
To where a rock forth issued from the bank.
That easily ascended, to the right
Upon its splinter turning, we depart
From those eternal barriers. When arriv'd,
Where underneath the gaping arch lets pass
The scourged souls: "Pause here," the teacher said,
"And let these others miserable, now
Strike on thy ken, faces not yet beheld,
For that together they with us have walk'd."

From the old bridge we ey'd the pack, who came
From th' other side towards us, like the rest,
Excoriate from the lash. My gentle guide,
By me unquestion'd, thus his speech resum'd:
"Behold that lofty shade, who this way tends,
And seems too woe-begone to drop a tear.
How yet the regal aspect he retains!
Jason is he, whose skill and prowess won
The ram from Colchos. To the Lemnian isle
His passage thither led him, when those bold
And pitiless women had slain all their males.
There he with tokens and fair witching words
Hypsipyle beguil'd, a virgin young,
Who first had all the rest herself beguil'd.
Impregnated he left her there forlorn.
Such is the guilt condemns him to this pain.
Here too Medea's inj'ries are avenged.
All bear him company, who like deceit
To his have practis'd. And thus much to know
Of the first vale suffice thee, and of those
Whom its keen torments urge." Now had we come
Where, crossing the next pier, the straighten'd path
Bestrides its shoulders to another arch.

Hence in the second chasm we heard the ghosts,
Who jibber in low melancholy sounds,
With wide-stretch'd nostrils snort, and on themselves
Smite with their palms. Upon the banks a scurf
From the foul steam condens'd, encrusting hung,
That held sharp combat with the sight and smell.

So hollow is the depth, that from no part,
Save on the summit of the rocky span,
Could I distinguish aught. Thus far we came;
And thence I saw, within the foss below,
A crowd immers'd in ordure, that appear'd
Draff of the human body. There beneath
Searching with eye inquisitive, I mark'd
One with his head so grim'd, 'twere hard to deem,
If he were clerk or layman. Loud he cried:
"Why greedily thus bendest more on me,
Than on these other filthy ones, thy ken?"

"Why greedily thus bendest more on me,
Than on these other filthy ones, thy ken?"
Canto XVIII, lines 116, 117.

"Because if true my mem'ry," I replied,
"I heretofore have seen thee with dry locks,
And thou Alessio art of Lucca sprung.
Therefore than all the rest I scan thee more."

Then beating on his brain these words he spake:
"Me thus low down my flatteries have sunk,
Wherewith I ne'er enough could glut my tongue."

My leader thus: "A little further stretch
Thy face, that thou the visage well mayst note
Of that besotted, sluttish courtezan,
Who there doth rend her with defiled nails,
Now crouching down, now risen on her feet.

"Thais is this, the harlot, whose false lip
Answer'd her doting paramour that ask'd,
'Thankest me much!'—'Say rather wondrously,'
And seeing this here satiate be our view."

CANTO XIX

    Woe to thee, Simon Magus! woe to you,
His wretched followers! who the things of God,
Which should be wedded unto goodness, them,
Rapacious as ye are, do prostitute
For gold and silver in adultery!
Now must the trumpet sound for you, since yours
Is the third chasm. Upon the following vault
We now had mounted, where the rock impends
Directly o'er the centre of the foss.

Wisdom Supreme! how wonderful the art,
Which thou dost manifest in heaven, in earth,
And in the evil world, how just a meed
Allotting by thy virtue unto all!

I saw the livid stone, throughout the sides
And in its bottom full of apertures,
All equal in their width, and circular each,
Nor ample less nor larger they appear'd
Than in Saint John's fair dome of me belov'd
Those fram'd to hold the pure baptismal streams,
One of the which I brake, some few years past,
To save a whelming infant; and be this
A seal to undeceive whoever doubts
The motive of my deed. From out the mouth
Of every one, emerg'd a sinner's feet
And of the legs high upward as the calf
The rest beneath was hid. On either foot
The soles were burning, whence the flexile joints
Glanc'd with such violent motion, as had snapt
Asunder cords or twisted withs. As flame,
Feeding on unctuous matter, glides along
The surface, scarcely touching where it moves;
So here, from heel to point, glided the flames.

"Master! say who is he, than all the rest
Glancing in fiercer agony, on whom
A ruddier flame doth prey?" I thus inquir'd.

"If thou be willing," he replied, "that I
Carry thee down, where least the slope bank falls,

He of himself shall tell thee and his wrongs."

I then: "As pleases thee to me is best.
Thou art my lord; and know'st that ne'er I quit
Thy will: what silence hides that knowest thou."
Thereat on the fourth pier we came, we turn'd,
And on our left descended to the depth,
A narrow strait and perforated close.
Nor from his side my leader set me down,
Till to his orifice he brought, whose limb
Quiv'ring express'd his pang. "Whoe'er thou art,
Sad spirit! thus revers'd, and as a stake
Driv'n in the soil!" I in these words began,
"If thou be able, utter forth thy voice."

There stood I like the friar, that doth shrive
A wretch for murder doom'd.
Canto XIX., lines 10, 11.

There stood I like the friar, that doth shrive
A wretch for murder doom'd, who e'en when fix'd,
Calleth him back, whence death awhile delays.

He shouted: "Ha! already standest there?
Already standest there, O Boniface!
By many a year the writing play'd me false.
So early dost thou surfeit with the wealth,
For which thou fearedst not in guile to take
The lovely lady, and then mangle her?"

I felt as those who, piercing not the drift
Of answer made them, stand as if expos'd
In mockery, nor know what to reply,
When Virgil thus admonish'd: "Tell him quick,
I am not he, not he, whom thou believ'st."

And I, as was enjoin'd me, straight replied.

That heard, the spirit all did wrench his feet,
And sighing next in woeful accent spake:
"What then of me requirest?" "If to know
So much imports thee, who I am, that thou
Hast therefore down the bank descended, learn
That in the mighty mantle I was rob'd,
And of a she-bear was indeed the son,
So eager to advance my whelps, that there
My having in my purse above I stow'd,
And here myself. Under my head are dragg'd
The rest, my predecessors in the guilt
Of simony. Stretch'd at their length they lie
Along an opening in the rock. 'Midst them
I also low shall fall, soon as he comes,
For whom I took thee, when so hastily
I question'd. But already longer time
Hath pass'd, since my souls kindled, and I thus
Upturn'd have stood, than is his doom to stand
Planted with fiery feet. For after him,
One yet of deeds more ugly shall arrive,
From forth the west, a shepherd without law,
Fated to cover both his form and mine.
He a new Jason shall be call'd, of whom
In Maccabees we read; and favour such

As to that priest his king indulgent show'd,
Shall be of France's monarch shown to him."

I know not if I here too far presum'd,
But in this strain I answer'd: "Tell me now,
What treasures from St. Peter at the first
Our Lord demanded, when he put the keys
Into his charge? Surely he ask'd no more
But, Follow me! Nor Peter nor the rest
Or gold or silver of Matthias took,
When lots were cast upon the forfeit place
Of the condemned soul. Abide thou then;
Thy punishment of right is merited:
And look thou well to that ill-gotten coin,
Which against Charles thy hardihood inspir'd.
If reverence of the keys restrain'd me not,
Which thou in happier time didst hold, I yet
Severer speech might use. Your avarice
O'ercasts the world with mourning, under foot
Treading the good, and raising bad men up.
Of shepherds, like to you, th' Evangelist
Was ware, when her, who sits upon the waves,
With kings in filthy whoredom he beheld,
She who with seven heads tower'd at her birth,
And from ten horns her proof of glory drew,
Long as her spouse in virtue took delight.
Of gold and silver ye have made your god,
Diff'ring wherein from the idolater,
But he that worships one, a hundred ye?
Ah, Constantine! to how much ill gave birth,
Not thy conversion, but that plenteous dower,
Which the first wealthy Father gain'd from thee!"

Meanwhile, as thus I sung, he, whether wrath
Or conscience smote him, violent upsprang
Spinning on either sole. I do believe
My teacher well was pleas'd, with so compos'd
A lip, he listen'd ever to the sound
Of the true words I utter'd. In both arms
He caught, and to his bosom lifting me
Upward retrac'd the way of his descent.

Nor weary of his weight he press'd me close,

Till to the summit of the rock we came,
Our passage from the fourth to the fifth pier.
His cherish'd burden there gently he plac'd
Upon the rugged rock and steep, a path
Not easy for the clamb'ring goat to mount.

Thence to my view another vale appear'd

CANTO XX

And now the verse proceeds to torments new,
Fit argument of this the twentieth strain
Of the first song, whose awful theme records
The spirits whelm'd in woe. Earnest I look'd
Into the depth, that open'd to my view,
Moisten'd with tears of anguish, and beheld
A tribe, that came along the hollow vale,
In silence weeping: such their step as walk
Quires chanting solemn litanies on earth.

As on them more direct mine eye descends,
Each wondrously seem'd to be revers'd
At the neck-bone, so that the countenance
Was from the reins averted: and because
None might before him look, they were compell'd
To' advance with backward gait. Thus one perhaps
Hath been by force of palsy clean transpos'd,
But I ne'er saw it nor believe it so.

Now, reader! think within thyself, so God
Fruit of thy reading give thee! how I long
Could keep my visage dry, when I beheld
Near me our form distorted in such guise,
That on the hinder parts fall'n from the face
The tears down-streaming roll'd. Against a rock
I leant and wept, so that my guide exclaim'd:
"What, and art thou too witless as the rest?
Here pity most doth show herself alive,
When she is dead. What guilt exceedeth his,
Who with Heaven's judgment in his passion strives?
Raise up thy head, raise up, and see the man,
Before whose eyes earth gap'd in Thebes, when all
Cried out, 'Amphiaraus, whither rushest?
'Why leavest thou the war?' He not the less
Fell ruining far as to Minos down,
Whose grapple none eludes. Lo! how he makes
The breast his shoulders, and who once too far
Before him wish'd to see, now backward looks,
And treads reverse his path. Tiresias note,
Who semblance chang'd, when woman he became
Of male, through every limb transform'd, and then

Once more behov'd him with his rod to strike
The two entwining serpents, ere the plumes,
That mark'd the better sex, might shoot again.

"Aruns, with more his belly facing, comes.
On Luni's mountains 'midst the marbles white,
Where delves Carrara's hind, who wons beneath,
A cavern was his dwelling, whence the stars
And main-sea wide in boundless view he held.

"The next, whose loosen'd tresses overspread
Her bosom, which thou seest not (for each hair
On that side grows) was Manto, she who search'd
Through many regions, and at length her seat
Fix'd in my native land, whence a short space
My words detain thy audience. When her sire
From life departed, and in servitude
The city dedicate to Bacchus mourn'd,
Long time she went a wand'rer through the world.
Aloft in Italy's delightful land
A lake there lies, at foot of that proud Alp,
That o'er the Tyrol locks Germania in,
Its name Benacus, which a thousand rills,
Methinks, and more, water between the vale
Camonica and Garda and the height
Of Apennine remote. There is a spot
At midway of that lake, where he who bears
Of Trento's flock the past'ral staff, with him
Of Brescia, and the Veronese, might each
Passing that way his benediction give.
A garrison of goodly site and strong
Peschiera stands, to awe with front oppos'd
The Bergamese and Brescian, whence the shore
More slope each way descends. There, whatsoev'er
Benacus' bosom holds not, tumbling o'er
Down falls, and winds a river flood beneath
Through the green pastures. Soon as in his course
The steam makes head, Benacus then no more
They call the name, but Mincius, till at last
Reaching Governo into Po he falls.
Not far his course hath run, when a wide flat
It finds, which overstretchmg as a marsh
It covers, pestilent in summer oft.

Hence journeying, the savage maiden saw
'Midst of the fen a territory waste
And naked of inhabitants. To shun
All human converse, here she with her slaves
Plying her arts remain'd, and liv'd, and left
Her body tenantless. Thenceforth the tribes,
Who round were scatter'd, gath'ring to that place
Assembled; for its strength was great, enclos'd
On all parts by the fen. On those dead bones
They rear'd themselves a city, for her sake,
Calling it Mantua, who first chose the spot,
Nor ask'd another omen for the name,
Wherein more numerous the people dwelt,
Ere Casalodi's madness by deceit
Was wrong'd of Pinamonte. If thou hear
Henceforth another origin assign'd
Of that my country, I forewarn thee now,
That falsehood none beguile thee of the truth."

I answer'd: "Teacher, I conclude thy words
So certain, that all else shall be to me
As embers lacking life. But now of these,
Who here proceed, instruct me, if thou see
Any that merit more especial note.
For thereon is my mind alone intent."

He straight replied: "That spirit, from whose cheek
The beard sweeps o'er his shoulders brown, what time
Graecia was emptied of her males, that scarce
The cradles were supplied, the seer was he
In Aulis, who with Calchas gave the sign
When first to cut the cable. Him they nam'd
Eurypilus: so sings my tragic strain,
In which majestic measure well thou know'st,
Who know'st it all. That other, round the loins
So slender of his shape, was Michael Scot,
Practis'd in ev'ry slight of magic wile.

"Guido Bonatti see: Asdente mark,
Who now were willing, he had tended still
The thread and cordwain; and too late repents.

"See next the wretches, who the needle left,

The shuttle and the spindle, and became
Diviners: baneful witcheries they wrought
With images and herbs. But onward now:
For now doth Cain with fork of thorns confine
On either hemisphere, touching the wave
Beneath the towers of Seville. Yesternight
The moon was round. Thou mayst remember well:
For she good service did thee in the gloom
Of the deep wood." This said, both onward mov'd.

CANTO XXI

Thus we from bridge to bridge, with other talk,
The which my drama cares not to rehearse,
Pass'd on; and to the summit reaching, stood
To view another gap, within the round
Of Malebolge, other bootless pangs.

Marvelous darkness shadow'd o'er the place.

In the Venetians' arsenal as boils
Through wintry months tenacious pitch, to smear
Their unsound vessels; for th' inclement time
Sea-faring men restrains, and in that while
His bark one builds anew, another stops
The ribs of his, that hath made many a voyage;
One hammers at the prow, one at the poop;
This shapeth oars, that other cables twirls,
The mizen one repairs and main-sail rent
So not by force of fire but art divine
Boil'd here a glutinous thick mass, that round
Lim'd all the shore beneath. I that beheld,
But therein nought distinguish'd, save the surge,
Rais'd by the boiling, in one mighty swell
Heave, and by turns subsiding and fall. While there
I fix'd my ken below, "Mark! mark!" my guide
Exclaiming, drew me towards him from the place,
Wherein I stood. I turn'd myself as one,
Impatient to behold that which beheld
He needs must shun, whom sudden fear unmans,
That he his flight delays not for the view.
Behind me I discern'd a devil black,
That running, up advanc'd along the rock.
Ah! what fierce cruelty his look bespake!
In act how bitter did he seem, with wings
Buoyant outstretch'd and feet of nimblest tread!
His shoulder proudly eminent and sharp
Was with a sinner charg'd; by either haunch
He held him, the foot's sinew griping fast.

"Ye of our bridge!" he cried, "keen-talon'd fiends!
Lo! one of Santa Zita's elders! Him
Whelm ye beneath, while I return for more.

That land hath store of such. All men are there,
Except Bonturo, barterers: of 'no'
For lucre there an 'aye' is quickly made."

Him dashing down, o'er the rough rock he turn'd,
Nor ever after thief a mastiff loos'd
Sped with like eager haste. That other sank
And forthwith writhing to the surface rose.
But those dark demons, shrouded by the bridge,
Cried "Here the hallow'd visage saves not: here
Is other swimming than in Serchio's wave.
Wherefore if thou desire we rend thee not,
Take heed thou mount not o'er the pitch." This said,
They grappled him with more than hundred hooks,
And shouted: "Cover'd thou must sport thee here;
So, if thou canst, in secret mayst thou filch."

This said,
They grappled him with more than hundred hooks.
Canto XXI., lines 50, 51.

E'en thus the cook bestirs him, with his grooms,
To thrust the flesh into the caldron down
With flesh-hooks, that it float not on the top.

Me then my guide bespake: "Lest they descry,
That thou art here, behind a craggy rock

Bend low and screen thee; and whate'er of force
Be offer'd me, or insult, fear thou not:
For I am well advis'd, who have been erst
In the like fray." Beyond the bridge's head
Therewith he pass'd, and reaching the sixth pier,
Behov'd him then a forehead terror-proof.

With storm and fury, as when dogs rush forth
Upon the poor man's back, who suddenly
From whence he standeth makes his suit; so rush'd
Those from beneath the arch, and against him
Their weapons all they pointed. He aloud:
"Be none of you outrageous: ere your time
Dare seize me, come forth from amongst you one,

"Be none of you outrageous."
Canto XXI, line 70.

"Who having heard my words, decide he then
If he shall tear these limbs." They shouted loud,
"Go, Malacoda!" Whereat one advanc'd,
The others standing firm, and as he came,
"What may this turn avail him?" he exclaim'd.

"Believ'st thou, Malacoda! I had come
Thus far from all your skirmishing secure,"

My teacher answered, "without will divine
And destiny propitious? Pass we then
For so Heaven's pleasure is, that I should lead
Another through this savage wilderness."

Forthwith so fell his pride, that he let drop
The instrument of torture at his feet,
And to the rest exclaim'd: "We have no power
To strike him." Then to me my guide: "O thou!
Who on the bridge among the crags dost sit
Low crouching, safely now to me return."

I rose, and towards him moved with speed: the fiends
Meantime all forward drew: me terror seiz'd
Lest they should break the compact they had made.
Thus issuing from Caprona, once I saw
Th' infantry dreading, lest his covenant
The foe should break; so close he hemm'd them round.

I to my leader's side adher'd, mine eyes
With fixt and motionless observance bent
On their unkindly visage. They their hooks
Protruding, one the other thus bespake:
"Wilt thou I touch him on the hip?" To whom
Was answer'd: "Even so; nor miss thy aim."

But he, who was in conf'rence with my guide,
Turn'd rapid round, and thus the demon spake:
"Stay, stay thee, Scarmiglione!" Then to us
He added: "Further footing to your step
This rock affords not, shiver'd to the base
Of the sixth arch. But would you still proceed,
Up by this cavern go: not distant far,
Another rock will yield you passage safe.
Yesterday, later by five hours than now,
Twelve hundred threescore years and six had fill'd
The circuit of their course, since here the way
Was broken. Thitherward I straight dispatch
Certain of these my scouts, who shall espy
If any on the surface bask. With them
Go ye: for ye shall find them nothing fell.
Come Alichino forth," with that he cried,
"And Calcabrina, and Cagnazzo thou!

The troop of ten let Barbariccia lead.
With Libicocco Draghinazzo haste,
Fang'd Ciriatto, Grafflacane fierce,
And Farfarello, and mad Rubicant.
Search ye around the bubbling tar. For these,
In safety lead them, where the other crag
Uninterrupted traverses the dens."

I then: "O master! what a sight is there!
Ah! without escort, journey we alone,
Which, if thou know the way, I covet not.
Unless thy prudence fail thee, dost not mark
How they do gnarl upon us, and their scowl
Threatens us present tortures?" He replied:
"I charge thee fear not: let them, as they will,
Gnarl on: 't is but in token of their spite
Against the souls, who mourn in torment steep'd."

To leftward o'er the pier they turn'd; but each
Had first between his teeth prest close the tongue,
Toward their leader for a signal looking,
Which he with sound obscene triumphant gave.

CANTO XXII

It hath been heretofore my chance to see
Horsemen with martial order shifting camp,
To onset sallying, or in muster rang'd,
Or in retreat sometimes outstretch'd for flight;
Light-armed squadrons and fleet foragers
Scouring thy plains, Arezzo! have I seen,
And clashing tournaments, and tilting jousts,
Now with the sound of trumpets, now of bells,
Tabors, or signals made from castled heights,
And with inventions multiform, our own,
Or introduc'd from foreign land; but ne'er
To such a strange recorder I beheld,
In evolution moving, horse nor foot,
Nor ship, that tack'd by sign from land or star.

With the ten demons on our way we went;
Ah fearful company! but in the church
With saints, with gluttons at the tavern's mess.

Still earnest on the pitch I gaz'd, to mark
All things whate'er the chasm contain'd, and those
Who burn'd within. As dolphins, that, in sign
To mariners, heave high their arched backs,
That thence forewarn'd they may advise to save
Their threaten'd vessels; so, at intervals,
To ease the pain his back some sinner show'd,
Then hid more nimbly than the lightning glance.

E'en as the frogs, that of a wat'ry moat
Stand at the brink, with the jaws only out,
Their feet and of the trunk all else concealed,
Thus on each part the sinners stood, but soon
As Barbariccia was at hand, so they
Drew back under the wave. I saw, and yet
My heart doth stagger, one, that waited thus,
As it befalls that oft one frog remains,
While the next springs away: and Graffiacan,
Who of the fiends was nearest, grappling seiz'd
His clotted locks, and dragg'd him sprawling up,
That he appear'd to me an otter. Each
Already by their names I knew, so well

When they were chosen, I observ'd, and mark'd
How one the other call'd. "O Rubicant!
See that his hide thou with thy talons flay,"
Shouted together all the cursed crew.

Then I: "Inform thee, master! if thou may,
What wretched soul is this, on whom their hand
His foes have laid." My leader to his side
Approach'd, and whence he came inquir'd, to whom
Was answer'd thus: "Born in Navarre's domain
My mother plac'd me in a lord's retinue,
For she had borne me to a losel vile,
A spendthrift of his substance and himself.
The good king Thibault after that I serv'd,
To peculating here my thoughts were turn'd,
Whereof I give account in this dire heat."

Straight Ciriatto, from whose mouth a tusk
Issued on either side, as from a boar,
Ript him with one of these. 'Twixt evil claws
The mouse had fall'n: but Barbariccia cried,
Seizing him with both arms: "Stand thou apart,
While I do fix him on my prong transpierc'd."
Then added, turning to my guide his face,
"Inquire of him, if more thou wish to learn,
Ere he again be rent." My leader thus:
"Then tell us of the partners in thy guilt;
Knowest thou any sprung of Latian land
Under the tar?"—"I parted," he replied,
"But now from one, who sojourn'd not far thence;
So were I under shelter now with him!
Nor hook nor talon then should scare me more."—.

"Too long we suffer," Libicocco cried,
Then, darting forth a prong, seiz'd on his arm,
And mangled bore away the sinewy part.
Him Draghinazzo by his thighs beneath
Would next have caught, whence angrily their chief,
Turning on all sides round, with threat'ning brow
Restrain'd them. When their strife a little ceas'd,
Of him, who yet was gazing on his wound,
My teacher thus without delay inquir'd:
"Who was the spirit, from whom by evil hap

Parting, as thou has told, thou cam'st to shore?"—

"It was the friar Gomita," he rejoin'd,
"He of Gallura, vessel of all guile,
Who had his master's enemies in hand,
And us'd them so that they commend him well.
Money he took, and them at large dismiss'd.
So he reports: and in each other charge
Committed to his keeping, play'd the part
Of barterer to the height: with him doth herd
The chief of Logodoro, Michel Zanche.
Sardinia is a theme, whereof their tongue
Is never weary. Out! alas! behold
That other, how he grins! More would I say,
But tremble lest he mean to maul me sore."

Their captain then to Farfarello turning,
Who roll'd his moony eyes in act to strike,
Rebuk'd him thus: "Off! cursed bird! Avaunt!"—

"If ye desire to see or hear," he thus
Quaking with dread resum'd, "or Tuscan spirits
Or Lombard, I will cause them to appear.
Meantime let these ill talons bate their fury,
So that no vengeance they may fear from them,
And I, remaining in this self-same place,
Will for myself but one, make sev'n appear,
When my shrill whistle shall be heard; for so
Our custom is to call each other up."

Cagnazzo at that word deriding grinn'd,
Then wagg'd the head and spake: "Hear his device,
Mischievous as he is, to plunge him down."

Whereto he thus, who fail'd not in rich store
Of nice-wove toils; "Mischief forsooth extreme,
Meant only to procure myself more woe!"

No longer Alichino then refrain'd,
But thus, the rest gainsaying, him bespake:
"If thou do cast thee down, I not on foot
Will chase thee, but above the pitch will beat
My plumes. Quit we the vantage ground, and let

The bank be as a shield, that we may see
If singly thou prevail against us all."

Now, reader, of new sport expect to hear!

They each one turn'd his eyes to the other shore,
He first, who was the hardest to persuade.
The spirit of Navarre chose well his time,
Planted his feet on land, and at one leap
Escaping disappointed their resolve.

Them quick resentment stung, but him the most,
Who was the cause of failure; in pursuit
He therefore sped, exclaiming: "Thou art caught."

In pursuit
He therefore sped, exclaiming, "Thou art caught."
Canto XXII, lines 125, 126.

 But little it avail'd: terror outstripp'd
His following flight: the other plung'd beneath,
And he with upward pinion rais'd his breast:
E'en thus the water-fowl, when she perceives
The falcon near, dives instant down, while he
Enrag'd and spent retires. That mockery
In Calcabrina fury stirr'd, who flew
After him, with desire of strife inflam'd;
And, for the barterer had 'scap'd, so turn'd

- 120 -

His talons on his comrade. O'er the dyke
In grapple close they join'd; but the other prov'd
A goshawk able to rend well his foe;

    And in the boiling lake both fell. The heat
Was umpire soon between them, but in vain
To lift themselves they strove, so fast were glued
Their pennons. Barbariccia, as the rest,
That chance lamenting, four in flight dispatch'd
From the other coast, with all their weapons arm'd.
They, to their post on each side speedily
Descending, stretch'd their hooks toward the fiends,
Who flounder'd, inly burning from their scars:
And we departing left them to that broil.

CANTO XXIII

In silence and in solitude we went,
One first, the other following his steps,
As minor friars journeying on their road.

The present fray had turn'd my thoughts to muse
Upon old Aesop's fable, where he told
What fate unto the mouse and frog befell.
For language hath not sounds more like in sense,
Than are these chances, if the origin
And end of each be heedfully compar'd.
And as one thought bursts from another forth,
So afterward from that another sprang,
Which added doubly to my former fear.
For thus I reason'd: "These through us have been
So foil'd, with loss and mock'ry so complete,
As needs must sting them sore. If anger then
Be to their evil will conjoin'd, more fell
They shall pursue us, than the savage hound
Snatches the leveret, panting 'twixt his jaws."

Already I perceiv'd my hair stand all
On end with terror, and look'd eager back.

"Teacher," I thus began, "if speedily
Thyself and me thou hide not, much I dread
Those evil talons. Even now behind
They urge us: quick imagination works
So forcibly, that I already feel them."

He answer'd: "Were I form'd of leaded glass,
I should not sooner draw unto myself
Thy outward image, than I now imprint
That from within. This moment came thy thoughts
Presented before mine, with similar act
And count'nance similar, so that from both
I one design have fram'd. If the right coast
Incline so much, that we may thence descend
Into the other chasm, we shall escape
Secure from this imagined pursuit."

He had not spoke his purpose to the end,

When I from far beheld them with spread wings
Approach to take us. Suddenly my guide
Caught me, ev'n as a mother that from sleep
Is by the noise arous'd, and near her sees
The climbing fires, who snatches up her babe
And flies ne'er pausing, careful more of him
Than of herself, that but a single vest
Clings round her limbs. Down from the jutting beach
Supine he cast him, to that pendent rock,
Which closes on one part the other chasm.

Never ran water with such hurrying pace
Adown the tube to turn a landmill's wheel,
When nearest it approaches to the spokes,
As then along that edge my master ran,
Carrying me in his bosom, as a child,
Not a companion. Scarcely had his feet
Reach'd to the lowest of the bed beneath,

Scarcely had his feet
Reach'd to the lowest of the bed beneath,
When over us the steep they reach'd.
Canto XXIII, lines 52—54

    When over us the steep they reach'd; but fear
In him was none; for that high Providence,
Which plac'd them ministers of the fifth foss,
Power of departing thence took from them all.

There in the depth we saw a painted tribe,
Who pac'd with tardy steps around, and wept,
Faint in appearance and o'ercome with toil.
Caps had they on, with hoods, that fell low down
Before their eyes, in fashion like to those
Worn by the monks in Cologne. Their outside
Was overlaid with gold, dazzling to view,
But leaden all within, and of such weight,
That Frederick's compar'd to these were straw.
Oh, everlasting wearisome attire!

We yet once more with them together turn'd
To leftward, on their dismal moan intent.
But by the weight oppress'd, so slowly came
The fainting people, that our company
Was chang'd at every movement of the step.

Whence I my guide address'd: "See that thou find
Some spirit, whose name may by his deeds be known,
And to that end look round thee as thou go'st."

Then one, who understood the Tuscan voice,
Cried after us aloud: "Hold in your feet,
Ye who so swiftly speed through the dusk air.
Perchance from me thou shalt obtain thy wish."

Whereat my leader, turning, me bespake:
"Pause, and then onward at their pace proceed."

I staid, and saw two Spirits in whose look
Impatient eagerness of mind was mark'd
To overtake me; but the load they bare
And narrow path retarded their approach.

Soon as arriv'd, they with an eye askance
Perus'd me, but spake not: then turning each
To other thus conferring said: "This one
Seems, by the action of his throat, alive.
And, be they dead, what privilege allows
They walk unmantled by the cumbrous stole?"

"Tuscan, who visitest
The college of the mourning hypocrites,
Disdain not to instruct us who thou art."
Canto XXIII, lines 92—94.

    Then thus to me: "Tuscan, who visitest
The college of the mourning hypocrites,
Disdain not to instruct us who thou art."

"By Arno's pleasant stream," I thus replied,
"In the great city I was bred and grew,
And wear the body I have ever worn.
but who are ye, from whom such mighty grief,
As now I witness, courseth down your cheeks?
What torment breaks forth in this bitter woe?"
"Our bonnets gleaming bright with orange hue,"
One of them answer'd, "are so leaden gross,
That with their weight they make the balances
To crack beneath them. Joyous friars we were,
Bologna's natives, Catalano I,
He Loderingo nam'd, and by thy land
Together taken, as men used to take
A single and indifferent arbiter,
To reconcile their strifes. How there we sped,
Gardingo's vicinage can best declare."

"O friars!" I began, "your miseries—"
But there brake off, for one had caught my eye,

Fix'd to a cross with three stakes on the ground:
He, when he saw me, writh'd himself, throughout
Distorted, ruffling with deep sighs his beard.
And Catalano, who thereof was 'ware,

    Thus spake: "That pierced spirit, whom intent
Thou view'st, was he who gave the Pharisees
Counsel, that it were fitting for one man
To suffer for the people. He doth lie
Transverse; nor any passes, but him first
Behoves make feeling trial how each weighs.
In straits like this along the foss are plac'd
The father of his consort, and the rest
Partakers in that council, seed of ill
And sorrow to the Jews." I noted then,

How Virgil gaz'd with wonder upon him,
Thus abjectly extended on the cross
In banishment eternal. To the friar
He next his words address'd: "We pray ye tell,
If so be lawful, whether on our right
Lies any opening in the rock, whereby
We both may issue hence, without constraint
On the dark angels, that compell'd they come
To lead us from this depth." He thus replied:
"Nearer than thou dost hope, there is a rock
From the next circle moving, which o'ersteps
Each vale of horror, save that here his cope
Is shatter'd. By the ruin ye may mount:
For on the side it slants, and most the height
Rises below." With head bent down awhile
My leader stood, then spake: "He warn'd us ill,
Who yonder hangs the sinners on his hook."

To whom the friar: "At Bologna erst
I many vices of the devil heard,
Among the rest was said, 'He is a liar,
And the father of lies!'" When he had spoke,
My leader with large strides proceeded on,
Somewhat disturb'd with anger in his look.

I therefore left the spirits heavy laden,
And following, his beloved footsteps mark'd.

CANTO XXIV

In the year's early nonage, when the sun
Tempers his tresses in Aquarius' urn,
And now towards equal day the nights recede,
When as the rime upon the earth puts on
Her dazzling sister's image, but not long
Her milder sway endures, then riseth up
The village hind, whom fails his wintry store,
And looking out beholds the plain around
All whiten'd, whence impatiently he smites
His thighs, and to his hut returning in,
There paces to and fro, wailing his lot,
As a discomfited and helpless man;
Then comes he forth again, and feels new hope
Spring in his bosom, finding e'en thus soon
The world hath chang'd its count'nance, grasps his crook,
And forth to pasture drives his little flock:
So me my guide dishearten'd when I saw
His troubled forehead, and so speedily
That ill was cur'd; for at the fallen bridge
Arriving, towards me with a look as sweet,
He turn'd him back, as that I first beheld
At the steep mountain's foot. Regarding well
The ruin, and some counsel first maintain'd
With his own thought, he open'd wide his arm
And took me up. As one, who, while he works,
Computes his labour's issue, that he seems
Still to foresee the effect, so lifting me
Up to the summit of one peak, he fix'd
His eye upon another. "Grapple that,"
Said he, "but first make proof, if it be such
As will sustain thee." For one capp'd with lead
This were no journey. Scarcely he, though light,
And I, though onward push'd from crag to crag,
Could mount. And if the precinct of this coast
Were not less ample than the last, for him
I know not, but my strength had surely fail'd.
But Malebolge all toward the mouth
Inclining of the nethermost abyss,
The site of every valley hence requires,
That one side upward slope, the other fall.

At length the point of our descent we reach'd
From the last flag: soon as to that arriv'd,
So was the breath exhausted from my lungs,
I could no further, but did seat me there.

"Now needs thy best of man;" so spake my guide:
"For not on downy plumes, nor under shade
Of canopy reposing, fame is won,
Without which whosoe'er consumes his days
Leaveth such vestige of himself on earth,
As smoke in air or foam upon the wave.
Thou therefore rise: vanish thy weariness
By the mind's effort, in each struggle form'd
To vanquish, if she suffer not the weight
Of her corporeal frame to crush her down.
A longer ladder yet remains to scale.
From these to have escap'd sufficeth not.
If well thou note me, profit by my words."

I straightway rose, and show'd myself less spent
Than I in truth did feel me. "On," I cried,
"For I am stout and fearless." Up the rock
Our way we held, more rugged than before,
Narrower and steeper far to climb. From talk
I ceas'd not, as we journey'd, so to seem
Least faint; whereat a voice from the other foss
Did issue forth, for utt'rance suited ill.
Though on the arch that crosses there I stood,
What were the words I knew not, but who spake
Seem'd mov'd in anger. Down I stoop'd to look,
But my quick eye might reach not to the depth
For shrouding darkness; wherefore thus I spake:
"To the next circle, Teacher, bend thy steps,
And from the wall dismount we; for as hence
I hear and understand not, so I see
Beneath, and naught discern."—"I answer not,"
Said he, "but by the deed. To fair request
Silent performance maketh best return."

We from the bridge's head descended, where
To the eighth mound it joins, and then the chasm
Opening to view, I saw a crowd within
Of serpents terrible, so strange of shape

And hideous, that remembrance in my veins
Yet shrinks the vital current. Of her sands
Let Lybia vaunt no more: if Jaculus,
Pareas and Chelyder be her brood,
Cenchris and Amphisboena, plagues so dire
Or in such numbers swarming ne'er she shew'd,
Not with all Ethiopia, and whate'er
Above the Erythraean sea is spawn'd.

Amid this dread exuberance of woe
Ran naked spirits wing'd with horrid fear,
Nor hope had they of crevice where to hide,
Or heliotrope to charm them out of view.
Canto XXIV, lines 87—92.

    Amid this dread exuberance of woe
Ran naked spirits wing'd with horrid fear,
Nor hope had they of crevice where to hide,
Or heliotrope to charm them out of view.
With serpents were their hands behind them bound,
Which through their reins infix'd the tail and head
Twisted in folds before. And lo! on one
Near to our side, darted an adder up,
And, where the neck is on the shoulders tied,
Transpierc'd him. Far more quickly than e'er pen
Wrote O or I, he kindled, burn'd, and chang'd
To ashes, all pour'd out upon the earth.
When there dissolv'd he lay, the dust again

Uproll'd spontaneous, and the self-same form
Instant resumed. So mighty sages tell,
The Arabian Phoenix, when five hundred years
Have well nigh circled, dies, and springs forthwith
Renascent. Blade nor herb throughout his life
He tastes, but tears of frankincense alone
And odorous amomum: swaths of nard
And myrrh his funeral shroud. As one that falls,
He knows not how, by force demoniac dragg'd
To earth, or through obstruction fettering up
In chains invisible the powers of man,
Who, risen from his trance, gazeth around,
Bewilder'd with the monstrous agony
He hath endur'd, and wildly staring sighs;
So stood aghast the sinner when he rose.

Oh! how severe God's judgment, that deals out
Such blows in stormy vengeance! Who he was
My teacher next inquir'd, and thus in few
He answer'd: "Vanni Fucci am I call'd,
Not long since rained down from Tuscany
To this dire gullet. Me the beastial life
And not the human pleas'd, mule that I was,
Who in Pistoia found my worthy den."

I then to Virgil: "Bid him stir not hence,
And ask what crime did thrust him hither: once
A man I knew him choleric and bloody."

The sinner heard and feign'd not, but towards me
His mind directing and his face, wherein
Was dismal shame depictur'd, thus he spake:
"It grieves me more to have been caught by thee
In this sad plight, which thou beholdest, than
When I was taken from the other life.
I have no power permitted to deny
What thou inquirest." I am doom'd thus low
To dwell, for that the sacristy by me
Was rifled of its goodly ornaments,
And with the guilt another falsely charged.
But that thou mayst not joy to see me thus,
So as thou e'er shalt 'scape this darksome realm
Open thine ears and hear what I forebode.

Reft of the Neri first Pistoia pines,
Then Florence changeth citizens and laws.
From Valdimagra, drawn by wrathful Mars,
A vapour rises, wrapt in turbid mists,
And sharp and eager driveth on the storm
With arrowy hurtling o'er Piceno's field,
Whence suddenly the cloud shall burst, and strike
Each helpless Bianco prostrate to the ground.
This have I told, that grief may rend thy heart."

CANTO XXV

When he had spoke, the sinner rais'd his hands
Pointed in mockery, and cried: "Take them, God!
I level them at thee!" From that day forth
The serpents were my friends; for round his neck
One of then rolling twisted, as it said,
"Be silent, tongue!" Another to his arms
Upgliding, tied them, riveting itself
So close, it took from them the power to move.

Pistoia! Ah Pistoia! why dost doubt
To turn thee into ashes, cumb'ring earth
No longer, since in evil act so far
Thou hast outdone thy seed? I did not mark,
Through all the gloomy circles of the abyss,
Spirit, that swell'd so proudly 'gainst his God,
Not him, who headlong fell from Thebes. He fled,
Nor utter'd more; and after him there came
A centaur full of fury, shouting, "Where
Where is the caitiff?" On Maremma's marsh
Swarm not the serpent tribe, as on his haunch
They swarm'd, to where the human face begins.
Behind his head upon the shoulders lay,
With open wings, a dragon breathing fire
On whomsoe'er he met. To me my guide:
"Cacus is this, who underneath the rock
Of Aventine spread oft a lake of blood.
He, from his brethren parted, here must tread
A different journey, for his fraudful theft
Of the great herd, that near him stall'd; whence found
His felon deeds their end, beneath the mace
Of stout Alcides, that perchance laid on
A hundred blows, and not the tenth was felt."

While yet he spake, the centaur sped away:
And under us three spirits came, of whom
Nor I nor he was ware, till they exclaim'd;
"Say who are ye?" We then brake off discourse,
Intent on these alone. I knew them not;
But, as it chanceth oft, befell, that one
Had need to name another. "Where," said he,
"Doth Cianfa lurk?" I, for a sign my guide

Should stand attentive, plac'd against my lips
The finger lifted. If, O reader! now
Thou be not apt to credit what I tell,
No marvel; for myself do scarce allow
The witness of mine eyes. But as I looked
Toward them, lo! a serpent with six feet
Springs forth on one, and fastens full upon him:
His midmost grasp'd the belly, a forefoot
Seiz'd on each arm (while deep in either cheek
He flesh'd his fangs); the hinder on the thighs
Were spread, 'twixt which the tail inserted curl'd
Upon the reins behind. Ivy ne'er clasp'd
A dodder'd oak, as round the other's limbs
The hideous monster intertwin'd his own.
Then, as they both had been of burning wax,
Each melted into other, mingling hues,
That which was either now was seen no more.
Thus up the shrinking paper, ere it burns,
A brown tint glides, not turning yet to black,
And the clean white expires. The other two
Look'd on exclaiming: "Ah, how dost thou change,
Agnello! See! Thou art nor double now,

The other two
Look'd on, exclaiming, "Ah! how dost thou change,
Agnello!
Canto XXV, lines 59—61.

"Nor only one." The two heads now became
One, and two figures blended in one form
Appear'd, where both were lost. Of the four lengths
Two arms were made: the belly and the chest
The thighs and legs into such members chang'd,
As never eye hath seen. Of former shape
All trace was vanish'd. Two yet neither seem'd
That image miscreate, and so pass'd on
With tardy steps. As underneath the scourge
Of the fierce dog-star, that lays bare the fields,
Shifting from brake to brake, the lizard seems
A flash of lightning, if he thwart the road,
So toward th' entrails of the other two
Approaching seem'd, an adder all on fire,
As the dark pepper-grain, livid and swart.
In that part, whence our life is nourish'd first,

One he transpierc'd; then down before him fell
Stretch'd out. The pierced spirit look'd on him
But spake not; yea stood motionless and yawn'd,
As if by sleep or fev'rous fit assail'd.
He ey'd the serpent, and the serpent him.
One from the wound, the other from the mouth
Breath'd a thick smoke, whose vap'ry columns join'd.

Lucan in mute attention now may hear,
Nor thy disastrous fate, Sabellus! tell,
Nor shine, Nasidius! Ovid now be mute.
What if in warbling fiction he record
Cadmus and Arethusa, to a snake
Him chang'd, and her into a fountain clear,
I envy not; for never face to face
Two natures thus transmuted did he sing,
Wherein both shapes were ready to assume
The other's substance. They in mutual guise
So answer'd, that the serpent split his train
Divided to a fork, and the pierc'd spirit
Drew close his steps together, legs and thighs
Compacted, that no sign of juncture soon
Was visible: the tail disparted took
The figure which the spirit lost, its skin
Soft'ning, his indurated to a rind.
The shoulders next I mark'd, that ent'ring join'd
The monster's arm-pits, whose two shorter feet
So lengthen'd, as the other's dwindling shrunk.
The feet behind then twisting up became
That part that man conceals, which in the wretch
Was cleft in twain. While both the shadowy smoke
With a new colour veils, and generates
Th' excrescent pile on one, peeling it off
From th' other body, lo! upon his feet
One upright rose, and prone the other fell.
Not yet their glaring and malignant lamps
Were shifted, though each feature chang'd beneath.
Of him who stood erect, the mounting face
Retreated towards the temples, and what there
Superfluous matter came, shot out in ears
From the smooth cheeks, the rest, not backward dragg'd,
Of its excess did shape the nose; and swell'd
Into due size protuberant the lips.

He, on the earth who lay, meanwhile extends
His sharpen'd visage, and draws down the ears
Into the head, as doth the slug his horns.
His tongue continuous before and apt
For utt'rance, severs; and the other's fork
Closing unites. That done the smoke was laid.
The soul, transform'd into the brute, glides off,
Hissing along the vale, and after him
The other talking sputters; but soon turn'd
His new-grown shoulders on him, and in few
Thus to another spake: "Along this path
Crawling, as I have done, speed Buoso now!"

So saw I fluctuate in successive change
Th' unsteady ballast of the seventh hold:
And here if aught my tongue have swerv'd, events
So strange may be its warrant. O'er mine eyes
Confusion hung, and on my thoughts amaze.

Yet 'scap'd they not so covertly, but well
I mark'd Sciancato: he alone it was
Of the three first that came, who chang'd not: thou,
The other's fate, Gaville, still dost rue.

CANTO XXVI

Florence exult! for thou so mightily
Hast thriven, that o'er land and sea thy wings
Thou beatest, and thy name spreads over hell!
Among the plund'rers such the three I found
Thy citizens, whence shame to me thy son,
And no proud honour to thyself redounds.

But if our minds, when dreaming near the dawn,
Are of the truth presageful, thou ere long
Shalt feel what Prato, (not to say the rest)
Would fain might come upon thee; and that chance
Were in good time, if it befell thee now.
Would so it were, since it must needs befall!
For as time wears me, I shall grieve the more.

We from the depth departed; and my guide
Remounting scal'd the flinty steps, which late
We downward trac'd, and drew me up the steep.
Pursuing thus our solitary way
Among the crags and splinters of the rock,
Sped not our feet without the help of hands.

Then sorrow seiz'd me, which e'en now revives,
As my thought turns again to what I saw,
And, more than I am wont, I rein and curb
The powers of nature in me, lest they run
Where Virtue guides not; that if aught of good
My gentle star, or something better gave me,
I envy not myself the precious boon.

As in that season, when the sun least veils
His face that lightens all, what time the fly
Gives way to the shrill gnat, the peasant then
Upon some cliff reclin'd, beneath him sees
Fire-flies innumerous spangling o'er the vale,
Vineyard or tilth, where his day-labour lies:
With flames so numberless throughout its space
Shone the eighth chasm, apparent, when the depth
Was to my view expos'd. As he, whose wrongs
The bears aveng'd, at its departure saw
Elijah's chariot, when the steeds erect

Rais'd their steep flight for heav'n; his eyes meanwhile,
Straining pursu'd them, till the flame alone
Upsoaring like a misty speck he kenn'd;
E'en thus along the gulf moves every flame,
A sinner so enfolded close in each,
That none exhibits token of the theft.

Upon the bridge I forward bent to look,
And grasp'd a flinty mass, or else had fall'n,
Though push'd not from the height. The guide, who mark'd
How I did gaze attentive, thus began:

The guide, who mark'd
How I did gaze attentive, thus began:
"Within these ardours are the spirits, each
Swathed in confining fire."
Canto XXVI., lines 46—49.

"Within these ardours are the spirits, each
Swath'd in confining fire."—"Master, thy word,"
I answer'd, "hath assur'd me; yet I deem'd

- 140 -

Already of the truth, already wish'd
To ask thee, who is in yon fire, that comes
So parted at the summit, as it seem'd
Ascending from that funeral pile, where lay
The Theban brothers?" He replied: "Within
Ulysses there and Diomede endure
Their penal tortures, thus to vengeance now
Together hasting, as erewhile to wrath.
These in the flame with ceaseless groans deplore
The ambush of the horse, that open'd wide
A portal for that goodly seed to pass,
Which sow'd imperial Rome; nor less the guile
Lament they, whence of her Achilles 'reft
Deidamia yet in death complains.
And there is rued the stratagem, that Troy
Of her Palladium spoil'd."—"If they have power
Of utt'rance from within these sparks," said I,
"O master! think my prayer a thousand fold
In repetition urg'd, that thou vouchsafe
To pause, till here the horned flame arrive.
See, how toward it with desire I bend."

He thus: "Thy prayer is worthy of much praise,
And I accept it therefore: but do thou
Thy tongue refrain: to question them be mine,
For I divine thy wish: and they perchance,
For they were Greeks, might shun discourse with thee."

When there the flame had come, where time and place
Seem'd fitting to my guide, he thus began:
"O ye, who dwell two spirits in one fire!
If living I of you did merit aught,
Whate'er the measure were of that desert,
When in the world my lofty strain I pour'd,
Move ye not on, till one of you unfold
In what clime death o'ertook him self-destroy'd."

Of the old flame forthwith the greater horn
Began to roll, murmuring, as a fire
That labours with the wind, then to and fro
Wagging the top, as a tongue uttering sounds,
Threw out its voice, and spake: "When I escap'd
From Circe, who beyond a circling year

Had held me near Caieta, by her charms,
Ere thus Aeneas yet had nam'd the shore,
Nor fondness for my son, nor reverence
Of my old father, nor return of love,
That should have crown'd Penelope with joy,
Could overcome in me the zeal I had
T' explore the world, and search the ways of life,
Man's evil and his virtue. Forth I sail'd
Into the deep illimitable main,
With but one bark, and the small faithful band
That yet cleav'd to me. As Iberia far,
Far as Morocco either shore I saw,
And the Sardinian and each isle beside
Which round that ocean bathes. Tardy with age
Were I and my companions, when we came
To the strait pass, where Hercules ordain'd
The bound'ries not to be o'erstepp'd by man.
The walls of Seville to my right I left,
On the other hand already Ceuta past.
"O brothers!" I began, "who to the west
Through perils without number now have reach'd,
To this the short remaining watch, that yet
Our senses have to wake, refuse not proof
Of the unpeopled world, following the track
Of Phoebus. Call to mind from whence we sprang:
Ye were not form'd to live the life of brutes
But virtue to pursue and knowledge high."
With these few words I sharpen'd for the voyage
The mind of my associates, that I then
Could scarcely have withheld them. To the dawn
Our poop we turn'd, and for the witless flight
Made our oars wings, still gaining on the left.
Each star of the other pole night now beheld,
And ours so low, that from the ocean-floor
It rose not. Five times re-illum'd, as oft
Vanish'd the light from underneath the moon
Since the deep way we enter'd, when from far
Appear'd a mountain dim, loftiest methought
Of all I e'er beheld. Joy seiz'd us straight,
But soon to mourning changed. From the new land
A whirlwind sprung, and at her foremost side
Did strike the vessel. Thrice it whirl'd her round
With all the waves, the fourth time lifted up

The poop, and sank the prow: so fate decreed:
And over us the booming billow clos'd."

CANTO XVII

Now upward rose the flame, and still'd its light
To speak no more, and now pass'd on with leave
From the mild poet gain'd, when following came
Another, from whose top a sound confus'd,
Forth issuing, drew our eyes that way to look.

As the Sicilian bull, that rightfully
His cries first echoed, who had shap'd its mould,
Did so rebellow, with the voice of him
Tormented, that the brazen monster seem'd
Pierc'd through with pain; thus while no way they found
Nor avenue immediate through the flame,
Into its language turn'd the dismal words:
But soon as they had won their passage forth,
Up from the point, which vibrating obey'd
Their motion at the tongue, these sounds we heard:
"O thou! to whom I now direct my voice!
That lately didst exclaim in Lombard phrase,

'Depart thou, I solicit thee no more,'
Though somewhat tardy I perchance arrive
Let it not irk thee here to pause awhile,
And with me parley: lo! it irks not me
And yet I burn. If but e'en now thou fall
into this blind world, from that pleasant land
Of Latium, whence I draw my sum of guilt,
Tell me if those, who in Romagna dwell,
Have peace or war. For of the mountains there
Was I, betwixt Urbino and the height,
Whence Tyber first unlocks his mighty flood."

Leaning I listen'd yet with heedful ear,
When, as he touch'd my side, the leader thus:
"Speak thou: he is a Latian." My reply
Was ready, and I spake without delay:

"O spirit! who art hidden here below!
Never was thy Romagna without war
In her proud tyrants' bosoms, nor is now:
But open war there left I none. The state,
Ravenna hath maintain'd this many a year,

Is steadfast. There Polenta's eagle broods,
And in his broad circumference of plume
O'ershadows Cervia. The green talons grasp
The land, that stood erewhile the proof so long,
And pil'd in bloody heap the host of France.

"The old mastiff of Verruchio and the young,
That tore Montagna in their wrath, still make,
Where they are wont, an augre of their fangs.

"Lamone's city and Santerno's range
Under the lion of the snowy lair.
Inconstant partisan! that changeth sides,
Or ever summer yields to winter's frost.
And she, whose flank is wash'd of Savio's wave,
As 'twixt the level and the steep she lies,
Lives so 'twixt tyrant power and liberty.

"Now tell us, I entreat thee, who art thou?
Be not more hard than others. In the world,
So may thy name still rear its forehead high."

Then roar'd awhile the fire, its sharpen'd point
On either side wav'd, and thus breath'd at last:
"If I did think, my answer were to one,
Who ever could return unto the world,
This flame should rest unshaken. But since ne'er,
If true be told me, any from this depth
Has found his upward way, I answer thee,
Nor fear lest infamy record the words.

"A man of arms at first, I cloth'd me then
In good Saint Francis' girdle, hoping so
T' have made amends. And certainly my hope
Had fail'd not, but that he, whom curses light on,
The high priest again seduc'd me into sin.
And how and wherefore listen while I tell.
Long as this spirit mov'd the bones and pulp
My mother gave me, less my deeds bespake
The nature of the lion than the fox.
All ways of winding subtlety I knew,
And with such art conducted, that the sound
Reach'd the world's limit. Soon as to that part

Of life I found me come, when each behoves
To lower sails and gather in the lines;
That which before had pleased me then I rued,
And to repentance and confession turn'd;
Wretch that I was! and well it had bested me!
The chief of the new Pharisees meantime,
Waging his warfare near the Lateran,
Not with the Saracens or Jews (his foes
All Christians were, nor against Acre one
Had fought, nor traffic'd in the Soldan's land),
He his great charge nor sacred ministry
In himself, rev'renc'd, nor in me that cord,
Which us'd to mark with leanness whom it girded.
As in Socrate, Constantine besought
To cure his leprosy Sylvester's aid,
So me to cure the fever of his pride
This man besought: my counsel to that end
He ask'd: and I was silent: for his words
Seem'd drunken: but forthwith he thus resum'd:
"From thy heart banish fear: of all offence
I hitherto absolve thee. In return,
Teach me my purpose so to execute,
That Penestrino cumber earth no more.
Heav'n, as thou knowest, I have power to shut
And open: and the keys are therefore twain,
The which my predecessor meanly priz'd."

Then, yielding to the forceful arguments,
Of silence as more perilous I deem'd,
And answer'd: "Father! since thou washest me
Clear of that guilt wherein I now must fall,
Large promise with performance scant, be sure,
Shall make thee triumph in thy lofty seat."

"When I was number'd with the dead, then came
Saint Francis for me; but a cherub dark
He met, who cried: "'Wrong me not; he is mine,
And must below to join the wretched crew,
For the deceitful counsel which he gave.
E'er since I watch'd him, hov'ring at his hair,
No power can the impenitent absolve;
Nor to repent and will at once consist,
By contradiction absolute forbid."

Oh mis'ry! how I shook myself, when he
Seiz'd me, and cried, "Thou haply thought'st me not
A disputant in logic so exact."
To Minos down he bore me, and the judge
Twin'd eight times round his callous back the tail,
Which biting with excess of rage, he spake:
'This is a guilty soul, that in the fire
Must vanish.' Hence perdition-doom'd I rove
A prey to rankling sorrow in this garb."

When he had thus fulfill'd his words, the flame
In dolour parted, beating to and fro,
And writhing its sharp horn. We onward went,
I and my leader, up along the rock,
Far as another arch, that overhangs
The foss, wherein the penalty is paid
Of those, who load them with committed sin.

CANTO XXVIII

Who, e'en in words unfetter'd, might at full
Tell of the wounds and blood that now I saw,
Though he repeated oft the tale? No tongue
So vast a theme could equal, speech and thought
Both impotent alike. If in one band
Collected, stood the people all, who e'er
Pour'd on Apulia's happy soil their blood,
Slain by the Trojans, and in that long war
When of the rings the measur'd booty made
A pile so high, as Rome's historian writes
Who errs not, with the multitude, that felt
The grinding force of Guiscard's Norman steel,
And those the rest, whose bones are gather'd yet
At Ceperano, there where treachery
Branded th' Apulian name, or where beyond
Thy walls, O Tagliacozzo, without arms
The old Alardo conquer'd; and his limbs
One were to show transpierc'd, another his
Clean lopt away; a spectacle like this
Were but a thing of nought, to the hideous sight
Of the ninth chasm. A rundlet, that hath lost
Its middle or side stave, gapes not so wide,
As one I mark'd, torn from the chin throughout
Down to the hinder passage: 'twixt the legs
Dangling his entrails hung, the midriff lay
Open to view, and wretched ventricle,
That turns th' englutted aliment to dross.

Whilst eagerly I fix on him my gaze,
He ey'd me, with his hands laid his breast bare,
And cried; "Now mark how I do rip me! lo!

"Now mark how I do rip me; lo!
How is Mahomet mangled."
Canto XXVIII, lines 30, 31

"How is Mohammed mangled! before me
Walks Ali weeping, from the chin his face
Cleft to the forelock; and the others all
Whom here thou seest, while they liv'd, did sow
Scandal and schism, and therefore thus are rent.
A fiend is here behind, who with his sword
Hacks us thus cruelly, slivering again
Each of this ream, when we have compast round
The dismal way, for first our gashes close
Ere we repass before him. But say who
Art thou, that standest musing on the rock,
Haply so lingering to delay the pain
Sentenc'd upon thy crimes?"—"Him death not yet,"
My guide rejoin'd, "hath overta'en, nor sin
Conducts to torment; but, that he may make

Full trial of your state, I who am dead
Must through the depths of hell, from orb to orb,
Conduct him. Trust my words, for they are true."

More than a hundred spirits, when that they heard,
Stood in the foss to mark me, through amazed,
Forgetful of their pangs. "Thou, who perchance
Shalt shortly view the sun, this warning thou
Bear to Dolcino: bid him, if he wish not
Here soon to follow me, that with good store
Of food he arm him, lest impris'ning snows
Yield him a victim to Novara's power,
No easy conquest else." With foot uprais'd
For stepping, spake Mohammed, on the ground
Then fix'd it to depart. Another shade,
Pierc'd in the throat, his nostrils mutilate
E'en from beneath the eyebrows, and one ear
Lopt off, who with the rest through wonder stood
Gazing, before the rest advanc'd, and bar'd
His wind-pipe, that without was all o'ersmear'd
With crimson stain. "O thou!" said 'he, "whom sin
Condemns not, and whom erst (unless too near
Resemblance do deceive me) I aloft
Have seen on Latian ground, call thou to mind
Piero of Medicina, if again
Returning, thou behold'st the pleasant land
That from Vercelli slopes to Mercabo;

Call thou to mind
Piero of Medicina, if again
Returning, thou behold'st the pleasant land
That from Vercelli slopes to Mercabò.
Canto XXVIII., lines 69—72.

"And there instruct the twain, whom Fano boasts
Her worthiest sons, Guido and Angelo,
That if 't is giv'n us here to scan aright
The future, they out of life's tenement
Shall be cast forth, and whelm'd under the waves
Near to Cattolica, through perfidy
Of a fell tyrant. 'Twixt the Cyprian isle
And Balearic, ne'er hath Neptune seen
An injury so foul, by pirates done
Or Argive crew of old. That one-ey'd traitor
(Whose realm there is a spirit here were fain
His eye had still lack'd sight of) them shall bring
To conf'rence with him, then so shape his end,
That they shall need not 'gainst Focara's wind
Offer up vow nor pray'r." I answering thus:

"Declare, as thou dost wish that I above
May carry tidings of thee, who is he,
In whom that sight doth wake such sad remembrance?"

Forthwith he laid his hand on the cheek-bone
Of one, his fellow-spirit, and his jaws

Expanding, cried: "Lo! this is he I wot of;
He speaks not for himself: the outcast this
Who overwhelm'd the doubt in Caesar's mind,
Affirming that delay to men prepar'd
Was ever harmful. "Oh how terrified
Methought was Curio, from whose throat was cut
The tongue, which spake that hardy word. Then one
Maim'd of each hand, uplifted in the gloom
The bleeding stumps, that they with gory spots
Sullied his face, and cried: 'Remember thee
Of Mosca, too, I who, alas! exclaim'd,
"The deed once done there is an end," that prov'd
A seed of sorrow to the Tuscan race."

I added: "Ay, and death to thine own tribe."

Whence heaping woe on woe he hurried off,
As one grief-stung to madness. But I there
Still linger'd to behold the troop, and saw
Things, such as I may fear without more proof
To tell of, but that conscience makes me firm,
The boon companion, who her strong breast-plate
Buckles on him, that feels no guilt within
And bids him on and fear not. Without doubt
I saw, and yet it seems to pass before me,
A headless trunk, that even as the rest
Of the sad flock pac'd onward. By the hair
It bore the sever'd member, lantern-wise
Pendent in hand, which look'd at us and said,

By the hair
It bore the sever'd member, lantern-wise
Pendent in hand, which look'd at us, and said,
"Woe's me!" *Canto XXVIII., lines 116—119.*

"Woe's me!" The spirit lighted thus himself,
And two there were in one, and one in two.
How that may be he knows who ordereth so.

When at the bridge's foot direct he stood,
His arm aloft he rear'd, thrusting the head
Full in our view, that nearer we might hear
The words, which thus it utter'd: "Now behold
This grievous torment, thou, who breathing go'st
To spy the dead; behold if any else
Be terrible as this. And that on earth
Thou mayst bear tidings of me, know that I
Am Bertrand, he of Born, who gave King John
The counsel mischievous. Father and son
I set at mutual war. For Absalom

And David more did not Ahitophel,
Spurring them on maliciously to strife.
For parting those so closely knit, my brain
Parted, alas! I carry from its source,
That in this trunk inhabits. Thus the law
Of retribution fiercely works in me."

CANTO XXIX

   So were mine eyes inebriate with view
Of the vast multitude, whom various wounds
Disfigur'd, that they long'd to stay and weep.

   But Virgil rous'd me: "What yet gazest on?
Wherefore doth fasten yet thy sight below
Among the maim'd and miserable shades?
Thou hast not shewn in any chasm beside
This weakness. Know, if thou wouldst number them
That two and twenty miles the valley winds
Its circuit, and already is the moon
Beneath our feet: the time permitted now
Is short, and more not seen remains to see."

"If thou," I straight replied, "hadst weigh'd the cause
For which I look'd, thou hadst perchance excus'd
The tarrying still." My leader part pursu'd
His way, the while I follow'd, answering him,
And adding thus: "Within that cave I deem,
Whereon so fixedly I held my ken,
There is a spirit dwells, one of my blood,
Wailing the crime that costs him now so dear."

Then spake my master: "Let thy soul no more
Afflict itself for him. Direct elsewhere
Its thought, and leave him. At the bridge's foot
I mark'd how he did point with menacing look
At thee, and heard him by the others nam'd
Geri of Bello. Thou so wholly then
Wert busied with his spirit, who once rul'd
The towers of Hautefort, that thou lookedst not
That way, ere he was gone."—"O guide belov'd!
His violent death yet unaveng'd," said I,
"By any, who are partners in his shame,
Made him contemptuous: therefore, as I think,
He pass'd me speechless by; and doing so
Hath made me more compassionate his fate."

So we discours'd to where the rock first show'd
The other valley, had more light been there,
E'en to the lowest depth. Soon as we came
O'er the last cloister in the dismal rounds
Of Malebolge, and the brotherhood
Were to our view expos'd, then many a dart
Of sore lament assail'd me, headed all
With points of thrilling pity, that I clos'd
Both ears against the volley with mine hands.

As were the torment, if each lazar-house
Of Valdichiana, in the sultry time
'Twixt July and September, with the isle
Sardinia and Maremma's pestilent fen,
Had heap'd their maladies all in one foss
Together; such was here the torment: dire
The stench, as issuing steams from fester'd limbs.

We on the utmost shore of the long rock
Descended still to leftward. Then my sight
Was livelier to explore the depth, wherein
The minister of the most mighty Lord,
All-searching Justice, dooms to punishment
The forgers noted on her dread record.

> Then my sight
> Was livelier to explore the depth, wherein
> The minister of the most mighty Lord,
> All-searching Justice, dooms to punishment
> The forgers noted on her dread record.
> *Canto XXIX., lines 52—56.*

    More rueful was it not methinks to see
The nation in Aegina droop, what time
Each living thing, e'en to the little worm,
All fell, so full of malice was the air
(And afterward, as bards of yore have told,
The ancient people were restor'd anew
From seed of emmets) than was here to see
The spirits, that languish'd through the murky vale

Up-pil'd on many a stack. Confus'd they lay,
One o'er the belly, o'er the shoulders one
Roll'd of another; sideling crawl'd a third
Along the dismal pathway. Step by step
We journey'd on, in silence looking round
And list'ning those diseas'd, who strove in vain
To lift their forms. Then two I mark'd, that sat
Propp'd 'gainst each other, as two brazen pans
Set to retain the heat. From head to foot,
A tetter bark'd them round. Nor saw I e'er
Groom currying so fast, for whom his lord
Impatient waited, or himself perchance
Tir'd with long watching, as of these each one
Plied quickly his keen nails, through furiousness
Of ne'er abated pruriency. The crust
Came drawn from underneath in flakes, like scales
Scrap'd from the bream or fish of broader mail.

The crust
Came drawn from underneath in flakes, like scales
scraped from the bream, or fish of broader mail.
Canto XXIX., lines 79—81.

"O thou, who with thy fingers rendest off
Thy coat of proof," thus spake my guide to one,
"And sometimes makest tearing pincers of them,
Tell me if any born of Latian land
Be among these within: so may thy nails

- 158 -

Serve thee for everlasting to this toil."

"Both are of Latium," weeping he replied,
"Whom tortur'd thus thou seest: but who art thou
That hast inquir'd of us?" To whom my guide:
"One that descend with this man, who yet lives,
From rock to rock, and show him hell's abyss."

Then started they asunder, and each turn'd
Trembling toward us, with the rest, whose ear
Those words redounding struck. To me my liege
Address'd him: "Speak to them whate'er thou list."

And I therewith began: "So may no time
Filch your remembrance from the thoughts of men
In th' upper world, but after many suns
Survive it, as ye tell me, who ye are,
And of what race ye come. Your punishment,
Unseemly and disgustful in its kind,
Deter you not from opening thus much to me."

"Arezzo was my dwelling," answer'd one,
"And me Albero of Sienna brought
To die by fire; but that, for which I died,
Leads me not here. True is in sport I told him,
That I had learn'd to wing my flight in air.
And he admiring much, as he was void
Of wisdom, will'd me to declare to him
The secret of mine art: and only hence,
Because I made him not a Daedalus,
Prevail'd on one suppos'd his sire to burn me.
But Minos to this chasm last of the ten,
For that I practis'd alchemy on earth,
Has doom'd me. Him no subterfuge eludes."

Then to the bard I spake: "Was ever race
Light as Sienna's? Sure not France herself
Can show a tribe so frivolous and vain."

The other leprous spirit heard my words,
And thus return'd: "Be Stricca from this charge
Exempted, he who knew so temp'rately
To lay out fortune's gifts; and Niccolo

Who first the spice's costly luxury
Discover'd in that garden, where such seed
Roots deepest in the soil: and be that troop
Exempted, with whom Caccia of Asciano
Lavish'd his vineyards and wide-spreading woods,
And his rare wisdom Abbagliato show'd
A spectacle for all. That thou mayst know
Who seconds thee against the Siennese
Thus gladly, bend this way thy sharpen'd sight,
That well my face may answer to thy ken;
So shalt thou see I am Capocchio's ghost,
Who forg'd transmuted metals by the power
Of alchemy; and if I scan thee right,
Thus needs must well remember how I aped
Creative nature by my subtle art."

CANTO XXX

What time resentment burn'd in Juno's breast
For Semele against the Theban blood,
As more than once in dire mischance was rued,
Such fatal frenzy seiz'd on Athamas,
That he his spouse beholding with a babe
Laden on either arm, "Spread out," he cried,
"The meshes, that I take the lioness
And the young lions at the pass:" then forth
Stretch'd he his merciless talons, grasping one,
One helpless innocent, Learchus nam'd,
Whom swinging down he dash'd upon a rock,
And with her other burden self-destroy'd
The hapless mother plung'd: and when the pride
Of all-presuming Troy fell from its height,
By fortune overwhelm'd, and the old king
With his realm perish'd, then did Hecuba,
A wretch forlorn and captive, when she saw
Polyxena first slaughter'd, and her son,
Her Polydorus, on the wild sea-beach
Next met the mourner's view, then reft of sense
Did she run barking even as a dog;
Such mighty power had grief to wrench her soul.
Bet ne'er the Furies or of Thebes or Troy
With such fell cruelty were seen, their goads
Infixing in the limbs of man or beast,
As now two pale and naked ghost I saw
That gnarling wildly scamper'd, like the swine
Excluded from his stye. One reach'd Capocchio,
And in the neck-joint sticking deep his fangs,
Dragg'd him, that o'er the solid pavement rubb'd
His belly stretch'd out prone. The other shape,
He of Arezzo, there left trembling, spake;
"That sprite of air is Schicchi; in like mood
Of random mischief vents he still his spite."

"That spirit of air is Schicchi; in like mood
Of random mischief vents he still his spite."
Canto XXX., lines 31, 34.

    To whom I answ'ring: "Oh! as thou dost hope,
The other may not flesh its jaws on thee,
Be patient to inform us, who it is,
Ere it speed hence."—"That is the ancient soul
Of wretched Myrrha," he replied, "who burn'd
With most unholy flame for her own sire,

"That is the ancient soul
Of wretched Myrrha."
Canto XXX. lines 38, 39.

"And a false shape assuming, so perform'd
The deed of sin; e'en as the other there,
That onward passes, dar'd to counterfeit
Donati's features, to feign'd testament
The seal affixing, that himself might gain,
For his own share, the lady of the herd."

When vanish'd the two furious shades, on whom
Mine eye was held, I turn'd it back to view
The other cursed spirits. One I saw
In fashion like a lute, had but the groin
Been sever'd, where it meets the forked part.
Swoln dropsy, disproportioning the limbs
With ill-converted moisture, that the paunch
Suits not the visage, open'd wide his lips
Gasping as in the hectic man for drought,

One towards the chin, the other upward curl'd.

"O ye, who in this world of misery,
Wherefore I know not, are exempt from pain,"
Thus he began, "attentively regard
Adamo's woe. When living, full supply
Ne'er lack'd me of what most I coveted;
One drop of water now, alas! I crave.
The rills, that glitter down the grassy slopes
Of Casentino, making fresh and soft
The banks whereby they glide to Arno's stream,
Stand ever in my view; and not in vain;
For more the pictur'd semblance dries me up,
Much more than the disease, which makes the flesh
Desert these shrivel'd cheeks. So from the place,
Where I transgress'd, stern justice urging me,
Takes means to quicken more my lab'ring sighs.
There is Romena, where I falsified
The metal with the Baptist's form imprest,
For which on earth I left my body burnt.
But if I here might see the sorrowing soul
Of Guido, Alessandro, or their brother,
For Branda's limpid spring I would not change
The welcome sight. One is e'en now within,
If truly the mad spirits tell, that round
Are wand'ring. But wherein besteads me that?
My limbs are fetter'd. Were I but so light,
That I each hundred years might move one inch,
I had set forth already on this path,
Seeking him out amidst the shapeless crew,
Although eleven miles it wind, not more
Than half of one across. They brought me down
Among this tribe; induc'd by them I stamp'd
The florens with three carats of alloy."

"Who are that abject pair," I next inquir'd,
"That closely bounding thee upon thy right
Lie smoking, like a band in winter steep'd
In the chill stream?"—"When to this gulf I dropt,"
He answer'd, "here I found them; since that hour
They have not turn'd, nor ever shall, I ween,
Till time hath run his course. One is that dame
The false accuser of the Hebrew youth;

Sinon the other, that false Greek from Troy.
Sharp fever drains the reeky moistness out,
In such a cloud upsteam'd." When that he heard,
One, gall'd perchance to be so darkly nam'd,
With clench'd hand smote him on the braced paunch,
That like a drum resounded: but forthwith
Adamo smote him on the face, the blow
Returning with his arm, that seem'd as hard.

"Though my o'erweighty limbs have ta'en from me
The power to move," said he, "I have an arm
At liberty for such employ." To whom
Was answer'd: "When thou wentest to the fire,
Thou hadst it not so ready at command,
Then readier when it coin'd th' impostor gold."

And thus the dropsied: "Ay, now speak'st thou true.
But there thou gav'st not such true testimony,
When thou wast question'd of the truth, at Troy."

"If I spake false, thou falsely stamp'dst the coin,"
Said Sinon; "I am here but for one fault,
And thou for more than any imp beside."

"Remember," he replied, "O perjur'd one,
The horse remember, that did teem with death,
And all the world be witness to thy guilt."

"To thine," return'd the Greek, "witness the thirst
Whence thy tongue cracks, witness the fluid mound,
Rear'd by thy belly up before thine eyes,
A mass corrupt." To whom the coiner thus:
"Thy mouth gapes wide as ever to let pass
Its evil saying. Me if thirst assails,
Yet I am stuff'd with moisture. Thou art parch'd,
Pains rack thy head, no urging would'st thou need
To make thee lap Narcissus' mirror up."

I was all fix'd to listen, when my guide
Admonish'd: "Now beware: a little more,
And I do quarrel with thee." I perceiv'd
How angrily he spake, and towards him turn'd
With shame so poignant, as remember'd yet

Confounds me. As a man that dreams of harm
Befall'n him, dreaming wishes it a dream,
And that which is, desires as if it were not,
Such then was I, who wanting power to speak
Wish'd to excuse myself, and all the while
Excus'd me, though unweeting that I did.

"More grievous fault than thine has been, less shame,"
My master cried, "might expiate. Therefore cast
All sorrow from thy soul; and if again
Chance bring thee, where like conference is held,
Think I am ever at thy side. To hear
Such wrangling is a joy for vulgar minds."

CANTO XXXI

The very tongue, whose keen reproof before
Had wounded me, that either cheek was stain'd,
Now minister'd my cure. So have I heard,
Achilles and his father's javelin caus'd
Pain first, and then the boon of health restor'd.

Turning our back upon the vale of woe,
W cross'd th' encircled mound in silence. There
Was twilight dim, that far long the gloom
Mine eye advanc'd not: but I heard a horn
Sounded aloud. The peal it blew had made
The thunder feeble. Following its course
The adverse way, my strained eyes were bent
On that one spot. So terrible a blast
Orlando blew not, when that dismal rout
O'erthrew the host of Charlemagne, and quench'd
His saintly warfare. Thitherward not long
My head was rais'd, when many lofty towers
Methought I spied. "Master," said I, "what land
Is this?" He answer'd straight: "Too long a space
Of intervening darkness has thine eye
To traverse: thou hast therefore widely err'd
In thy imagining. Thither arriv'd
Thou well shalt see, how distance can delude
The sense. A little therefore urge thee on."

Then tenderly he caught me by the hand;
"Yet know," said he, "ere farther we advance,
That it less strange may seem, these are not towers,
But giants. In the pit they stand immers'd,
Each from his navel downward, round the bank."

As when a fog disperseth gradually,
Our vision traces what the mist involves
Condens'd in air; so piercing through the gross
And gloomy atmosphere, as more and more
We near'd toward the brink, mine error fled,
And fear came o'er me. As with circling round
Of turrets, Montereggion crowns his walls,
E'en thus the shore, encompassing th' abyss,
Was turreted with giants, half their length

- 167 -

Uprearing, horrible, whom Jove from heav'n
Yet threatens, when his mutt'ring thunder rolls.

Of one already I descried the face,
Shoulders, and breast, and of the belly huge
Great part, and both arms down along his ribs.

All-teeming nature, when her plastic hand
Left framing of these monsters, did display
Past doubt her wisdom, taking from mad War
Such slaves to do his bidding; and if she
Repent her not of th' elephant and whale,
Who ponders well confesses her therein
Wiser and more discreet; for when brute force
And evil will are back'd with subtlety,
Resistance none avails. His visage seem'd
In length and bulk, as doth the pine, that tops
Saint Peter's Roman fane; and th' other bones
Of like proportion, so that from above
The bank, which girdled him below, such height
Arose his stature, that three Friezelanders
Had striv'n in vain to reach but to his hair.
Full thirty ample palms was he expos'd
Downward from whence a man his garments loops.
"Raphel bai ameth sabi almi,"
So shouted his fierce lips, which sweeter hymns
Became not; and my guide address'd him thus:

"O senseless spirit! let thy horn for thee
Interpret: therewith vent thy rage, if rage
Or other passion wring thee. Search thy neck,
There shalt thou find the belt that binds it on.
Wild spirit! lo, upon thy mighty breast
Where hangs the baldrick!" Then to me he spake:
"He doth accuse himself. Nimrod is this,
Through whose ill counsel in the world no more
One tongue prevails. But pass we on, nor waste
Our words; for so each language is to him,
As his to others, understood by none."

Then to the leftward turning sped we forth,
And at a sling's throw found another shade
Far fiercer and more huge. I cannot say

What master hand had girt him; but he held
Behind the right arm fetter'd, and before
The other with a chain, that fasten'd him
From the neck down, and five times round his form
Apparent met the wreathed links. "This proud one
Would of his strength against almighty Jove
Make trial," said my guide; "whence he is thus
Requited: Ephialtes him they call.

"This proud one
Would of his strength against almighty Jove
Make trial."   *Canto XXXI. lines 82—84*

"Great was his prowess, when the giants brought
Fear on the gods: those arms, which then he piled,
Now moves he never." Forthwith I return'd:
"Fain would I, if 't were possible, mine eyes
Of Briareus immeasurable gain'd
Experience next." He answer'd: "Thou shalt see
Not far from hence Antaeus, who both speaks
And is unfetter'd, who shall place us there
Where guilt is at its depth. Far onward stands
Whom thou wouldst fain behold, in chains, and made
Like to this spirit, save that in his looks
More fell he seems." By violent earthquake rock'd
Ne'er shook a tow'r, so reeling to its base,
As Ephialtes. More than ever then

I dreaded death, nor than the terror more
Had needed, if I had not seen the cords
That held him fast. We, straightway journeying on,
Came to Antaeus, who five ells complete
Without the head, forth issued from the cave.

"O thou, who in the fortunate vale, that made
Great Scipio heir of glory, when his sword
Drove back the troop of Hannibal in flight,
Who thence of old didst carry for thy spoil
An hundred lions; and if thou hadst fought
In the high conflict on thy brethren's side,
Seems as men yet believ'd, that through thine arm
The sons of earth had conquer'd, now vouchsafe
To place us down beneath, where numbing cold
Locks up Cocytus. Force not that we crave
Or Tityus' help or Typhon's. Here is one
Can give what in this realm ye covet. Stoop
Therefore, nor scornfully distort thy lip.
He in the upper world can yet bestow
Renown on thee, for he doth live, and looks
For life yet longer, if before the time
Grace call him not unto herself." Thus spake
The teacher. He in haste forth stretch'd his hands,
And caught my guide. Alcides whilom felt
That grapple straighten'd score. Soon as my guide
Had felt it, he bespake me thus: "This way
That I may clasp thee;" then so caught me up,
That we were both one burden. As appears
The tower of Carisenda, from beneath
Where it doth lean, if chance a passing cloud
So sail across, that opposite it hangs,
Such then Antaeus seem'd, as at mine ease
I mark'd him stooping. I were fain at times
T' have pass'd another way. Yet in th' abyss,
That Lucifer with Judas low ingulfs,
lightly he plac'd us; nor there leaning stay'd,
But rose as in a bark the stately mast.

Yet in the abyss,
That Lucifer with Judas low ingulfs,
Lightly he placed us.
Canto XXXI, lines 133—135.

CANTO XXXII

    Could I command rough rhimes and hoarse, to suit
That hole of sorrow, o'er which ev'ry rock
His firm abutment rears, then might the vein
Of fancy rise full springing: but not mine
Such measures, and with falt'ring awe I touch
The mighty theme; for to describe the depth
Of all the universe, is no emprize
To jest with, and demands a tongue not us'd
To infant babbling. But let them assist
My song, the tuneful maidens, by whose aid
Amphion wall'd in Thebes, so with the truth
My speech shall best accord. Oh ill-starr'd folk,
Beyond all others wretched! who abide
In such a mansion, as scarce thought finds words
To speak of, better had ye here on earth
Been flocks or mountain goats. As down we stood
In the dark pit beneath the giants' feet,
But lower far than they, and I did gaze
Still on the lofty battlement, a voice
Bespoke me thus: "Look how thou walkest. Take
Good heed, thy soles do tread not on the heads
Of thy poor brethren." Thereupon I turn'd,
And saw before and underneath my feet
A lake, whose frozen surface liker seem'd
To glass than water. Not so thick a veil
In winter e'er hath Austrian Danube spread
O'er his still course, nor Tanais far remote
Under the chilling sky. Roll'd o'er that mass
Had Tabernich or Pietrapana fall'n,

"Look how thou walkest. Take
Good heed, thy soles do tread not on the heads
Of thy poor brethren."
Canto XXXII, lines 20—22.

    Not e'en its rim had creak'd. As peeps the frog
Croaking above the wave, what time in dreams
The village gleaner oft pursues her toil,
So, to where modest shame appears, thus low
Blue pinch'd and shrin'd in ice the spirits stood,
Moving their teeth in shrill note like the stork.
His face each downward held; their mouth the cold,
Their eyes express'd the dolour of their heart.

A space I look'd around, then at my feet
Saw two so strictly join'd, that of their head
The very hairs were mingled. "Tell me ye,
Whose bosoms thus together press," said I,
"Who are ye?" At that sound their necks they bent,
And when their looks were lifted up to me,
Straightway their eyes, before all moist within,
Distill'd upon their lips, and the frost bound
The tears betwixt those orbs and held them there.
Plank unto plank hath never cramp clos'd up
So stoutly. Whence like two enraged goats
They clash'd together; them such fury seiz'd.

And one, from whom the cold both ears had reft,

Exclaim'd, still looking downward: "Why on us
Dost speculate so long? If thou wouldst know
Who are these two, the valley, whence his wave
Bisenzio slopes, did for its master own
Their sire Alberto, and next him themselves.
They from one body issued; and throughout
Caina thou mayst search, nor find a shade
More worthy in congealment to be fix'd,
Not him, whose breast and shadow Arthur's land
At that one blow dissever'd, not Focaccia,
No not this spirit, whose o'erjutting head
Obstructs my onward view: he bore the name
Of Mascheroni: Tuscan if thou be,
Well knowest who he was: and to cut short
All further question, in my form behold
What once was Camiccione. I await
Carlino here my kinsman, whose deep guilt
Shall wash out mine." A thousand visages
Then mark'd I, which the keen and eager cold
Had shap'd into a doggish grin; whence creeps
A shiv'ring horror o'er me, at the thought
Of those frore shallows. While we journey'd on
Toward the middle, at whose point unites
All heavy substance, and I trembling went
Through that eternal chillness, I know not
If will it were or destiny, or chance,
But, passing 'midst the heads, my foot did strike
With violent blow against the face of one.

"Wherefore dost bruise me?" weeping, he exclaim'd,
"Unless thy errand be some fresh revenge
For Montaperto, wherefore troublest me?"

I thus: "Instructor, now await me here,
That I through him may rid me of my doubt.
Thenceforth what haste thou wilt." The teacher paus'd,
And to that shade I spake, who bitterly
Still curs'd me in his wrath. "What art thou, speak,
That railest thus on others?" He replied:
"Now who art thou, that smiting others' cheeks
Through Antenora roamest, with such force
As were past suff'rance, wert thou living still?"

"And I am living, to thy joy perchance,"
Was my reply, "if fame be dear to thee,
That with the rest I may thy name enrol."

"The contrary of what I covet most,"
Said he, "thou tender'st: hence; nor vex me more.
Ill knowest thou to flatter in this vale."

Then seizing on his hinder scalp I cried:
"Name thee, or not a hair shall tarry here!"
Canto XXXII, lines 97, 98.

Then seizing on his hinder scalp, I cried:
"Name thee, or not a hair shall tarry here."

"Rend all away," he answer'd, "yet for that
I will not tell nor show thee who I am,
Though at my head thou pluck a thousand times."

Now I had grasp'd his tresses, and stript off
More than one tuft, he barking, with his eyes
Drawn in and downward, when another cried,
"What ails thee, Bocca? Sound not loud enough
Thy chatt'ring teeth, but thou must bark outright?
"What devil wrings thee?"—"Now," said I, "be dumb,
Accursed traitor! to thy shame of thee
True tidings will I bear."—"Off," he replied,

- 176 -

"Tell what thou list; but as thou escape from hence
To speak of him whose tongue hath been so glib,
Forget not: here he wails the Frenchman's gold.
'Him of Duera,' thou canst say, 'I mark'd,
Where the starv'd sinners pine.' If thou be ask'd
What other shade was with them, at thy side
Is Beccaria, whose red gorge distain'd
The biting axe of Florence. Farther on,
If I misdeem not, Soldanieri bides,
With Ganellon, and Tribaldello, him
Who op'd Faenza when the people slept."

We now had left him, passing on our way,
When I beheld two spirits by the ice
Pent in one hollow, that the head of one
Was cowl unto the other; and as bread
Is raven'd up through hunger, th' uppermost
Did so apply his fangs to th' other's brain,
Where the spine joins it. Not more furiously
On Menalippus' temples Tydeus gnaw'd,
Than on that skull and on its garbage he.

Not more furiously
On Menalippus' temples Tydeus gnaw'd,
Than on that skull and on its garbage he.
Canto XXXII, lines 127–129

"O thou who show'st so beastly sign of hate
'Gainst him thou prey'st on, let me hear," said I
"The cause, on such condition, that if right
Warrant thy grievance, knowing who ye are,
And what the colour of his sinning was,
I may repay thee in the world above,
If that wherewith I speak be moist so long."

CANTO XXXIII

His jaws uplifting from their fell repast,
That sinner wip'd them on the hairs o' th' head,
Which he behind had mangled, then began:
"Thy will obeying, I call up afresh
Sorrow past cure, which but to think of wrings
My heart, or ere I tell on't. But if words,
That I may utter, shall prove seed to bear
Fruit of eternal infamy to him,
The traitor whom I gnaw at, thou at once
Shalt see me speak and weep. Who thou mayst be
I know not, nor how here below art come:
But Florentine thou seemest of a truth,
When I do hear thee. Know I was on earth
Count Ugolino, and th' Archbishop he
Ruggieri. Why I neighbour him so close,
Now list. That through effect of his ill thoughts
In him my trust reposing, I was ta'en
And after murder'd, need is not I tell.
What therefore thou canst not have heard, that is,
How cruel was the murder, shalt thou hear,
And know if he have wrong'd me. A small grate
Within that mew, which for my sake the name
Of famine bears, where others yet must pine,
Already through its opening sev'ral moons
Had shown me, when I slept the evil sleep,
That from the future tore the curtain off.
This one, methought, as master of the sport,
Rode forth to chase the gaunt wolf and his whelps
Unto the mountain, which forbids the sight
Of Lucca to the Pisan. With lean brachs
Inquisitive and keen, before him rang'd
Lanfranchi with Sismondi and Gualandi.
After short course the father and the sons
Seem'd tir'd and lagging, and methought I saw
The sharp tusks gore their sides. When I awoke
Before the dawn, amid their sleep I heard
My sons (for they were with me) weep and ask
For bread. Right cruel art thou, if no pang
Thou feel at thinking what my heart foretold;
And if not now, why use thy tears to flow?
Now had they waken'd; and the hour drew near

When they were wont to bring us food; the mind
Of each misgave him through his dream, and I
Heard, at its outlet underneath lock'd up
The horrible tower: whence uttering not a word
I look'd upon the visage of my sons.
I wept not: so all stone I felt within.
They wept: and one, my little Anslem, cried:
'Thou lookest so! Father what ails thee?' Yet
I shed no tear, nor answer'd all that day
Nor the next night, until another sun
Came out upon the world. When a faint beam
Had to our doleful prison made its way,
And in four countenances I descry'd
The image of my own, on either hand
Through agony I bit, and they who thought
I did it through desire of feeding, rose
O' th' sudden, and cried, 'Father, we should grieve
Far less, if thou wouldst eat of us: thou gav'st
These weeds of miserable flesh we wear,

*Then, not to make them sadder, I kept down
My spirit in stillness.*
Canto XXXIII, lines 62, 63

And do thou strip them off from us again.'
Then, not to make them sadder, I kept down
My spirit in stillness. That day and the next

- 180 -

We all were silent. Ah, obdurate earth!
Why open'dst not upon us? When we came
To the fourth day, then Geddo at my feet
Outstretch'd did fling him, crying, 'Hast no help
For me, my father!' There he died, and e'en
Plainly as thou seest me, saw I the three
Fall one by one 'twixt the fifth day and sixth:

"Hast no help
For me, my father?"
Canto XXXIII, lines 67, 68.

Whence I betook me now grown blind to grope
Over them all, and for three days aloud
Call'd on them who were dead. Then fasting got
The mastery of grief." Thus having spoke,

Once more upon the wretched skull his teeth
He fasten'd, like a mastiff's 'gainst the bone
Firm and unyielding. Oh thou Pisa! shame
Of all the people, who their dwelling make
In that fair region, where th' Italian voice
Is heard, since that thy neighbours are so slack
To punish, from their deep foundations rise
Capraia and Gorgona, and dam up
The mouth of Arno, that each soul in thee
May perish in the waters! What if fame
Reported that thy castles were betray'd
By Ugolino, yet no right hadst thou
To stretch his children on the rack. For them,
Brigata, Ugaccione, and the pair
Of gentle ones, of whom my song hath told,
Their tender years, thou modern Thebes! did make
Uncapable of guilt. Onward we pass'd,
Where others skarf'd in rugged folds of ice
Not on their feet were turn'd, but each revers'd.

There very weeping suffers not to weep;
For at their eyes grief seeking passage finds
Impediment, and rolling inward turns

For increase of sharp anguish: the first tears
Hang cluster'd, and like crystal vizors show,
Under the socket brimming all the cup.

Now though the cold had from my face dislodg'd
Each feeling, as 't were callous, yet me seem'd
Some breath of wind I felt. "Whence cometh this,"
Said I, "my master? Is not here below
All vapour quench'd?"—"Thou shalt be speedily,"
He answer'd, "where thine eye shall tell thee whence
The cause descrying of this airy shower."

Then cried out one in the chill crust who mourn'd:
"O souls so cruel! that the farthest post
Hath been assign'd you, from this face remove
The harden'd veil, that I may vent the grief
Impregnate at my heart, some little space
Ere it congeal again!" I thus replied:
"Say who thou wast, if thou wouldst have mine aid;
And if I extricate thee not, far down
As to the lowest ice may I descend!"

"The friar Alberigo," answered he,
"Am I, who from the evil garden pluck'd
Its fruitage, and am here repaid, the date
More luscious for my fig."—"Hah!" I exclaim'd,
"Art thou too dead!"—"How in the world aloft
It fareth with my body," answer'd he,
"I am right ignorant. Such privilege
Hath Ptolomea, that ofttimes the soul
Drops hither, ere by Atropos divorc'd.
And that thou mayst wipe out more willingly
The glazed tear-drops that o'erlay mine eyes,
Know that the soul, that moment she betrays,
As I did, yields her body to a fiend
Who after moves and governs it at will,
Till all its time be rounded; headlong she
Falls to this cistern. And perchance above
Doth yet appear the body of a ghost,
Who here behind me winters. Him thou know'st,
If thou but newly art arriv'd below.
The years are many that have pass'd away,
Since to this fastness Branca Doria came."

"Now," answer'd I, "methinks thou mockest me,
For Branca Doria never yet hath died,
But doth all natural functions of a man,
Eats, drinks, and sleeps, and putteth raiment on."

He thus: "Not yet unto that upper foss
By th' evil talons guarded, where the pitch
Tenacious boils, had Michael Zanche reach'd,
When this one left a demon in his stead
In his own body, and of one his kin,
Who with him treachery wrought. But now put forth
Thy hand, and ope mine eyes." I op'd them not.
Ill manners were best courtesy to him.

Ah Genoese! men perverse in every way,
With every foulness stain'd, why from the earth
Are ye not cancel'd? Such an one of yours
I with Romagna's darkest spirit found,
As for his doings even now in soul
Is in Cocytus plung'd, and yet doth seem
In body still alive upon the earth.

CANTO XXXIV

"The banners of Hell's Monarch do come forth
Towards us; therefore look," so spake my guide,
"If thou discern him." As, when breathes a cloud
Heavy and dense, or when the shades of night
Fall on our hemisphere, seems view'd from far
A windmill, which the blast stirs briskly round,
Such was the fabric then methought I saw,

To shield me from the wind, forthwith I drew
Behind my guide: no covert else was there.

Now came I (and with fear I bid my strain
Record the marvel) where the souls were all
Whelm'd underneath, transparent, as through glass
Pellucid the frail stem. Some prone were laid,
Others stood upright, this upon the soles,
That on his head, a third with face to feet
Arch'd like a bow. When to the point we came,
Whereat my guide was pleas'd that I should see
The creature eminent in beauty once,
He from before me stepp'd and made me pause.

"Lo!" he exclaim'd, "lo Dis! and lo the place,
Where thou hast need to arm thy heart with strength."

How frozen and how faint I then became,
Ask me not, reader! for I write it not,
Since words would fail to tell thee of my state.
I was not dead nor living. Think thyself
If quick conception work in thee at all,
How I did feel. That emperor, who sways
The realm of sorrow, at mid breast from th' ice
Stood forth; and I in stature am more like
A giant, than the giants are in his arms.
Mark now how great that whole must be, which suits
With such a part. If he were beautiful
As he is hideous now, and yet did dare
To scowl upon his Maker, well from him
May all our mis'ry flow. Oh what a sight!
How passing strange it seem'd, when I did spy
Upon his head three faces: one in front
Of hue vermilion, th' other two with this
Midway each shoulder join'd and at the crest;
The right 'twixt wan and yellow seem'd: the left
To look on, such as come from whence old Nile
Stoops to the lowlands. Under each shot forth
Two mighty wings, enormous as became
A bird so vast. Sails never such I saw
Outstretch'd on the wide sea. No plumes had they,
But were in texture like a bat, and these
He flapp'd i' th' air, that from him issued still
Three winds, wherewith Cocytus to its depth
Was frozen. At six eyes he wept: the tears
Adown three chins distill'd with bloody foam.
At every mouth his teeth a sinner champ'd
Bruis'd as with pond'rous engine, so that three
Were in this guise tormented. But far more
Than from that gnawing, was the foremost pang'd
By the fierce rending, whence ofttimes the back
Was stript of all its skin. "That upper spirit,
Who hath worse punishment," so spake my guide,
"Is Judas, he that hath his head within
And plies the feet without. Of th' other two,
Whose heads are under, from the murky jaw
Who hangs, is Brutus: lo! how he doth writhe

And speaks not! Th' other Cassius, that appears
So large of limb. But night now re-ascends,
And it is time for parting. All is seen."

I clipp'd him round the neck, for so he bade;
And noting time and place, he, when the wings
Enough were op'd, caught fast the shaggy sides,
And down from pile to pile descending stepp'd
Between the thick fell and the jagged ice.

Soon as he reach'd the point, whereat the thigh
Upon the swelling of the haunches turns,
My leader there with pain and struggling hard
Turn'd round his head, where his feet stood before,
And grappled at the fell, as one who mounts,
That into hell methought we turn'd again.

"Expect that by such stairs as these," thus spake
The teacher, panting like a man forespent,
"We must depart from evil so extreme."
Then at a rocky opening issued forth,
And plac'd me on a brink to sit, next join'd
With wary step my side. I rais'd mine eyes,
Believing that I Lucifer should see
Where he was lately left, but saw him now
With legs held upward. Let the grosser sort,
Who see not what the point was I had pass'd,
Bethink them if sore toil oppress'd me then.

"Arise," my master cried, "upon thy feet.
The way is long, and much uncouth the road;
And now within one hour and half of noon
The sun returns." It was no palace-hall
Lofty and luminous wherein we stood,
But natural dungeon where ill footing was
And scant supply of light. "Ere from th' abyss
I sep'rate," thus when risen I began,
"My guide! vouchsafe few words to set me free
From error's thralldom. Where is now the ice?
How standeth he in posture thus revers'd?
And how from eve to morn in space so brief
Hath the sun made his transit?" He in few
Thus answering spake: "Thou deemest thou art still

On th' other side the centre, where I grasp'd
Th' abhorred worm, that boreth through the world.
Thou wast on th' other side, so long as I
Descended; when I turn'd, thou didst o'erpass
That point, to which from ev'ry part is dragg'd
All heavy substance. Thou art now arriv'd
Under the hemisphere opposed to that,
Which the great continent doth overspread,
And underneath whose canopy expir'd
The Man, that was born sinless, and so liv'd.
Thy feet are planted on the smallest sphere,
Whose other aspect is Judecca. Morn
Here rises, when there evening sets: and he,
Whose shaggy pile was scal'd, yet standeth fix'd,
As at the first. On this part he fell down
From heav'n; and th' earth, here prominent before,
Through fear of him did veil her with the sea,
And to our hemisphere retir'd. Perchance
To shun him was the vacant space left here
By what of firm land on this side appears,
That sprang aloof." There is a place beneath,
From Belzebub as distant, as extends
The vaulted tomb, discover'd not by sight,
But by the sound of brooklet, that descends
This way along the hollow of a rock,
Which, as it winds with no precipitous course,
The wave hath eaten. By that hidden way
My guide and I did enter, to return
To the fair world: and heedless of repose
We climbed, he first, I following his steps,
Till on our view the beautiful lights of heav'n
Dawn'd through a circular opening in the cave:
Thus issuing we again beheld the stars.

By that hidden way
My guide and I did enter, to return
To the fair world.
Canto XXXIV, lines 127—129.

Thence issuing we again beheld the stars.
Canto XXXIV., line 133.

www.ingramcontent.com/pod-product-compliance
Ingram Content Group UK Ltd.
Pitfield, Milton Keynes, MK11 3LW, UK
UKHW020306120125
453409UK00004BA/254